# Draw Disciples

## James Harvey & Brian Hayden

# DRAW DISCIPLES

JAMES HARVEY & BRIAN HAYDEN

## Dedication

To the return of our Messiah King Jesus!

#Maranatha

# Contents

Foreward by Rob Harvey
Preface
Acknowledgements
Instructions
Maranatha Prayer

**Lessons**

**Resources**

Storytellers Game
Storytellers Book
Authors
Blazing Trees
Recommendations

# Foreward

Draw Disciples is a storytelling project.

These discipleship lessons were born from a longing to create resources that make Bible storytelling easy for everyone. We believe the Bible was given to the whole world, and these living words were breathed out to be heard and received by everyone on earth.

As highly text-reliant Westerners, how are we going to effectively pass along God's story of hope, healing, and restoration to oral peoples? Fortunately, we have the example Jesus models for us in the Gospels. Jesus is the perfect teacher for anyone considering oral Bible communication strategies for unreached peoples.

What did Jesus do? The storyteller culture of Jesus is remarkable. He used oral means to train his disciples, and he did not cut corners. Remember? The disciples Jesus trained from humble beginnings impressed even the leading scholars of their day. These disciples went on to use the same methods of Jesus to train others, resulting in a rapidly-expanding storyteller movement.

What can we do? We can use simple drawings of Bible stories that anyone can create. These are drawings any tribe can easily reproduce and adapt as the Holy Spirit guides them to relate Bible stories to their own indigenous cultures. We can share God's Word through these stories with every people and language, clearing the pathway for disciple making movements.

Recently, we partnered with a movement leader in India to create simple drawings for reaching Buddhists with the gospel. These drawings were then used to equip a pan-Asian gathering of church planters from over 20 nations. These story drawings streamlined the leadership development process and provided practices that leaders rapidly passed on to their teams.

We are companions alongside a church planting initiative currently engaging an unreached people group with less than 1% believers. With the ever-present threat of intense persecution, followers of Jesus can draw stories on napkins at a tea house or with someone met while prayer walking. We rejoice as we receive ongoing reports of these stories being shared and then passed along to more families and friends.

Apparently, Jesus knew what modern research confirms. If you want to achieve maximum impact, you must communicate in the hidden heart languages of the hearers. If you desire enduring fruit, you must engage the systems operating within each culture.

The Orality Bible project is a gift for this season. These lessons structure the Word of God for remembrance and multiplication. The simplicity of Draw Disciples conceals its effectiveness in overcoming our ethnocentric approach to communication and connection to people within their frame of reference.

Rob Harvey
CEO, Mission Advisors
missionadvisors.org

# Preface

Once upon a time, I was walking my dog while deeply conflicted in my spirit. For five years, I led gospel mission projects in Nashville, Tennessee: one of the most multicultural cities in America. Though our city is small, we are home to refugees and immigrants from 80 nations who speak over 100 languages every day. God desires everyone in our city to meet Jesus and adopt them as his children.

I continued to wrestle with God in prayer asking, "Father, how are we going to teach the nations here how to make disciples if many of them do not read or write in any language?" I had been serving the Lord in the Kurdish community and discovered in almost every home at least one person illiterate in both Arabic and English. "Father," I cried, "we need resources that your people living in many nations can use to tell your stories and make disciples of everyone who has yet to hear about Jesus and follow him!"

God graciously answered with a vision of the future. As I walked down the road listening to worship music on my phone, I saw God open up the sky, and a river began slowly flowing from heaven to earth. The river water fell in waves of every color of the rainbow and filled with hundreds of beautiful pictures and simple drawings. The Holy Spirit spoke clearly to me, "This river represents the future of discipleship. Our Father wants you to recruit a team and develop story resources using simple drawings that will not need to be translated into any languages. These are the resources you have requested that anyone can use in any language or level of education. These storyteller drawings are what your generation needs to reach the nations."

Hallelujah! I was relieved. I had seen examples of drawings like the vision I received in India and China, but never on the scale I felt the Lord leading me to create. I purchased oralitybible.com and reached out to Brian Hayden, our

Creative Director, to share the vision. We celebrated this answered prayer, began developing the drawings, and published them online for free. Our first story was the Lost Son in Luke 15, and we have continued creating these storyteller lessons as the Holy Spirit teaches us what to do.

This project has been an unpredictable adventure since the first story lesson. Our greatest challenge has been discerning how to present these resources in such a way that anyone feels confident using them. We desire to equip storytellers who will disciple others to become storytellers.

Enter our Draw Disciples book. This resource is the result of three years of project development. We have collected twenty lessons for teaching disciples about the kingdom of heaven directly from the Scriptures. We are confident that these drawings are all you need to expose your disciples to the Bible and coach them to develop their own disciples.

The title "Draw Disciples" has two meanings. First, we are disciples who practice drawing stories from the Bible with simple sketches. We want to remember every story and share God's Word with anyone the Lord plants in our paths. Second, Jesus draws new disciples to himself as we share the gospel. He said in John 12:32 that if we will lift him up, he will draw all nations to himself. We believe him, and we want every disciple to develop the skills of walking in the Holy Spirit and telling Jesus' stories to their neighbors.

We believe these storyteller resources will capture your heart with God's glory and inspire you to gather others to pray, draw stories, and join our generation's mission to take Jesus' gospel to every tribe until our Messiah King returns.

Welcome to the storyteller movement. Maranatha! Come quickly, Lord Jesus!

James Harvey

## Acknowledgments

We are so thankful for the love, support, and generosity of our family and friends. You have poured your lives into ours as we have learned how to develop disciples. Thank you.

Thank you to our amazing wives Jen Harvey and Jennifer Hayden for all the faithful love, prayers, and support. Thank you Jen for serving as our manuscript editor extraordinaire.

Thank you to our awesome kids Aiden, Jackson, Sophia, and Greyson for inspiring us in so many incredible ways.

Thank you Mark & Judy Harvey, Jim & Val Harvey, Sally Ozment, and Tommy & Carol Sanders for your faithfulness to follow God as he leads and raise families of disciples.

Thank you Terry Seelow, Dan Mihaila, and Doug Plumlee for inviting young men to cut their teeth on real ministry.

Thank you Nick Werline, Jay & Marcia Franks, and Chuck & Stacy Yungkurth for your legendary generosity.

David Kaufmann, you created spaces for investigating and experimenting with all these lessons in Nashville's streets.

Howard Everett, you fueled into flame this book with your stories, challenges, and audacious faith in what God will do.

Don Buege, this book would not exist without those nine hours in Indianapolis and the Tunka Valley mission vision.

Jan Esterline, this book would not exist without all our discussions about having absolutely no expectations.

Neill Mims, this book would not exist without those nine hours you spent drawing mission strategies in Singapore.

Jeff Sundell, this book would not exist without those scores of iron-on-iron whiteboard sessions and conversations.

Kumar Goshen, this book would not exist without our cup of tea with the prepared receiver at the bicycle shop in India.

Thank you to our close ministry friends for exploring these lessons with us over countless phone calls and digital meetings: Samuel Gautam, Tre Baugues, Adam Moma, Aaron Moma, Walt Dowdy, Clay Hamrick, and Ryan Wade.

Thank you No Place Left network friends for living out missions in the harvest fields for us to witness: Ray Vaughn, Troy Cooper, Carter Cox, Clint Harrill, Zach Medlock, Ron Surgeon, Casey & Nastasha Laws, and Chuck & Deb Wood.

Thank you Ying & Grace Kai for the three thirds discipleship process that we adapted in our Instructions for gatherings.

Thank you Nathan & Kari Shank for introducing us to the No Place Left vision and four fields strategy.

Thank you Steve Addison for your stellar storytelling about the miraculous movements of God throughout history.

Thank you Russell Moore for your exquisite research and profound teaching on the cosmic kingdom of Jesus Christ.

Thank you Aaron Palmquist for the fire house resource that we adapted in our Fire House lesson.

Thank you Neil Cole and Curtis Sergeant for your inspired discipleship DNA woven throughout these lessons.

Thank you Jimmy Scroggins for the 3 circles gospel resource that we adapted in our Salvation Freedom lesson.

**"If a story is in you, it has to come out." - William Faulkner**

Rest: flame & arrow - Our greatest need will always be to rest in Jesus and be refreshed in his living water presence. Activities in this part include sharing meals, praise, prayer, confessing struggles, healing, and encouragement.

Receive: cloud & rainbow - Rest and renewal open up our hearts to receive God's Word. The Bible overflows with hundreds of living, breathing stories. Activities in this part include reading the story, listening to the story, drawing and telling the story, discussing the story questions, and prayer.

Release: wave & water - Processing God's Word in our minds opens up our lives to practice whatever we learn. We receive stories and then release them to others as the Holy Spirit guides. Activities in this part include praying in faith for all nations, discussing our local communities, evaluating our mission strategies, and creating a plan to speak stories.

We clearly witness this pattern in the story of Jesus discipling Zacchaeus at his home. In Luke 19:1-10, Jesus visits Zacchaeus' village and invites himself over for a meal. Jesus and Zacchaeus enjoy rest during a home fellowship meal. Next, Jesus teaches his new disciple about the kingdom of heaven and guides him to experience the Holy

Spirit's presence. Then, Zacchaeus believes Jesus' stories and creates a simple plan to release generous gifts.

Each lesson has five sections that are easy to follow:

1. Discover - a brief overview of the lesson
2. Draw - a basic walkthrough of the story with drawings
3. Discuss - discovery questions to process with others
4. Disciple - practical questions to personally apply
5. Dedicate - a covenant prayer of faith

This book is designed as a practical resource for various disciple making venues:

• Personal Devotion
• Family Worship
• Master/apprentice spiritual skills development
• Small Groups & House Churches
• Leadership Teams
• Preaching Series
• Conference Sessions

We believe this resource will help you build the biblical foundation every disciple needs to faithfully follow Jesus.

We have adapted Ying & Grace Kai's three-thirds discipleship pattern (t4tglobalmissions.org) into our own style called "Rest, Receive, Release." This technique is also deeply influenced by Curtis Sergeant's GC2 structure of God's Commands and Great Commission (obeygc2.com).

All of our artwork and lessons are available free for download on our resource website: oralitybible.com

We have produced short training videos for all 20 lessons available for free on our Blazing Trees YouTube channel.

Questions? Please visit our website: blazingtrees.org

## Maranatha Prayer

Father, we love you! Blessed be the name of the Lord! Blessed is he who comes in the name of the Lord! Glory, glory, hallelujah! Hosanna in the highest! Maranatha!

Father, you made a way where there was no way for all creation to come home. Our home is wherever you are. You are our Abba Father, and we are your sons and daughters adopted out of earth's cursed orphanage into your eternal splendor. We do not have words to describe your amazing love. Who is able to write a song that captures your glory?

All the swirling galaxies scattered across our immeasurable universe move and breathe, and discover their identity and purpose alone in you. You are our Creator, the Lord of heaven and earth. Our planet is your footstool, and all the stars have sung your praises since creation's first breath.

You know every hair on each of our heads, and you name every star. You count every grain of sand, and you measure every drop of water in the oceans. We will never know you fully, for you are infinitely powerful and mysteriously wise. We surrender in faith and rest in your amazing grace.

Speak, Lord, for your servants are listening. We seek first your kingdom and righteousness, keeping our eyes fixed always upon you. You are the Ancient of Days, our Faithful Shepherd and Wonderful Counselor, our Risen Glory King.

Jesus, you are Heaven's Missionary. You came to seek the lost and save those forsaken in darkness and bondage. We declare salvation over every tribe, in Jesus' name and for his glory we pray, amen.

13

# Faithful Shepherd
## Psalms 23

## Discover

Faith is a strong belief and total confidence in someone. Faithful means trustworthy, loyal, and steadfast. A shepherd is someone who provides spiritual care and wise guidance.

Moses was a shepherd for many years. He learned how to guide and protect flocks of helpless animals, which prepared him to guide the helpless nation of Israel out of Egyptian slavery into the Promised Land. (Exodus 3:1-10)

King David was once a shepherd as a youth. His experience killing lions and bears to protect his sheep prepared him for battle with the dangerous giant Goliath. (1 Samuel 17:34-37)

Isaiah describes God as an affectionate shepherd who gently nurtures lambs, gathers wandering sheep together, and holds them close to his heart. (Isaiah 40:11)

Jesus called himself the Good Shepherd who protects the sheep from thieves and wolves. The sheep know his voice, and he willingly dies for the sake of his sheep. He even leaves his flock to rescue forsaken sheep. (John 10:11-18)

Paul gathered together the Ephesian church elders to pray before he left for Rome. He called them "shepherds," described their church as a "flock," and warned them that false teachers are like bloodthirsty wolves. (Acts 20:28-32)

This lesson teaches us about God Almighty's loving compassion and powerful protection. He is present in our lives, never leaving or forsaking us. Because God is so awesome and faithful, we trust him. We gladly endure suffering, persecution, and even death, because our Father is worthy of all honor, glory, and praise. (Revelation 4:9-11)

# FAITHFUL SHEPHERD

## PSALMS 23

# Draw

Devoted Protector: shepherd & sheep - King David describes our relationship with God as a shepherd caring for sheep. Sheep are dumb and defenseless. A shepherd watches over, provides for, and guides the sheep. (23:1)

Soul Restoration: tree, stream, & disciple - God loves and delights in us when we rest in him. He creates spaces and places for us to step back from the busyness of daily life to rest from our work, sing, pray, and listen to his voice. (23:2)

Refreshed Disciple: praising disciple & flag - All power and glory in the universe belong to God. He knows everything. Rest leads to trust, and trust leads to peace. Peaceful rest is the open door to hearing God and discerning his will. (23:3)

Suffering Seasons: valley & flames - We must expect suffering, because we follow a Master of Sorrows (Isaiah 53). Our peace and joy are knowing and experiencing the Holy Spirit as we journey through pain by faith. (23:4)

Safe House: rod, staff, & table - God is like a safe house: somewhere secure you can go when you are in trouble. His staff guides our steps, his rod defends against enemies, and his table is always set with triumphant victory. (23:4-5)

Divine Favor: cup, water, & overflow - The result of resting in God is receiving his blessings and favor. He showers us with spiritual gifts and assists us in serving others out of the overflow of whatever we have received. (23:5)

Heavenly Home: king, disciple, & house - When we surrender to our Saving Shepherd's leadership, his life becomes our life. We return his love, and his goodness flows through us like a river. This age will end soon, and we will live with God and his family forever in heaven. (23:6)

## Discuss

Psalms 23 begins and ends with examples of comforting rest, like green pastures and eternity in heaven. The middle of the song describes a death valley, evil forces, and dangerous enemies. Why do you think David wrote about God's refreshing rest in the context of spiritual warfare?

Take a closer look at this song. What does our Faithful Shepherd do? (example: he leads me) What do we do? (example: I will live) What stands out to you about the relationship between what God does and what we do?

Read Hebrews 13:20-21. Why is Jesus the "Great Shepherd?" He equips us with good things to do his will. What are some good things he equips us with to obey him? How does our faithfulness bring him eternal glory?

Read 1 Peter 2:21-25. How is it possible for Jesus Christ to be both sheep and shepherd? When was he the sheep? When was he the shepherd? Compare your life as a straying sheep to a safe sheep secure in the Master's flock.

## Disciple

Let's get practical. Have you completely embraced this truth that God is your Faithful Shepherd who loves you, died to save you, and guides you through every day of your life? Pray, and speak to God about his loving protection over your life. Whom do you know that does not know God this way? When can you meet with them to discuss this song?

## Dedicate

Father, thank you for this glorious news that we can trust you to faithfully care for us. You are more than enough for all of our needs. We rest in your protection and receive your blessings, in Jesus' name and for his glory we pray, amen.

# Glory Hallelujah
Psalms 103

## Discover

Glory is the great beauty and royal majesty of God that causes our singing and dancing, our praising and praying. Hallelujah means "praise the Lord!" We speak this word as a public and personal sign of our participation in worship.

Our Father heals the brokenhearted; he gently cures our wounds. We praise him, because he created all the stars and gave names to each one. We praise him, because his power is limitless, his wisdom is boundless, and he lifts up the humble, raising them above the wicked. (Psalms 147:3-7)

Hannah calls God "the Most High." He seats the homeless beside princes, raises the dead, protects the weak, guards the faithful, and judges the nations. (1 Samuel 2:1-10)

Isaiah calls God "the Guiding Light to the Nations." He reveals his righteousness through his faithfulness, guards and protects us, lights up the darkness, opens blind eyes, and delivers captives out of dungeons. (Isaiah 42:6-7)

Daniel calls God "the Ancient of Days." His kingdom is holy, his dominion is everlasting, his power overcomes all wickedness and death, and all peoples, nations, and languages will praise his name. (Daniel 7:13-14)

Paul calls God "the Father of Compassion." He has compassion on mankind and sent Jesus to rescue us. He is the God of all Comfort who journeys alongside us through painful suffering and challenging trials. (2 Corinthians 1:3-4)

This lesson will stoke the fire of your passion to worship God. He is worthy of all honor, glory, and praise. Let us praise the Lord day and night forever! (Psalms 145:1-2)

# GLORY HALLELUJAH

## PSALMS 103

# Draw

Joyful Praise: worshipers & flags - Our first service to our Father is praise and worship. Our Creator designed us to praise him. We praise him with all of our hearts and souls. We sing praises to him and remember who he is. (103:1-2)

Surefire Deliverance: broken chain - God forgives our sin, repairs our broken bodies, and rescues us out of hell. God is just, and his justice is perfect. He overcomes oppression, defeats persecution, and liberates slaves. (103:3-4,6)

Steadfast Freedom: bird & crown - We were once slaves to rebellion against God's leadership; now in Christ, we are free forever. He satisfies us in ways no one else can. He crowns us with love, mercy, and grace. (103:4-5,8)

Indescribable Love: mountain & stars - God's great love surpasses the distance between the earth and the stars. Our Father is the Surgical Sin Extractor; he casts out our wickedness, commanding it never to return. He baptizes our souls with new life and amazing grace. (103:11-13)

Brief Lifetime: plant & wind - King David compares the immeasurable glory of God with mankind's mortality. We are fragile people living in a vast universe. We are alive for one breath of eternity, so let us remain humble. (103:14-16)

Blessed Descendants: generations & crown - When we decide to follow Jesus and become his disciples, we open the door to our ancestral line, welcoming his blessings and protection over our children and grandchildren. (103:17-18)

Faithful Angels: warrior angel - The Bible describes several spiritual realms coexisting with the earthly realm where we live. God's angels praise him. All the holy beings and supernatural species he has created praise him. Everything belongs to our God; let all creation praise him! (103:19-22)

## Discuss

Read Psalms 103:2-13 and make a list of everything God does for us. When you hear about God's faithfulness and intentional love, how do you feel? How have you experienced one or more of these awe-inspiring works?

Read Psalms 103:13-18. How do we "keep" a covenant with God? How does our personal devotion to God affect our descendants? What is one specific way you can model your dedication to God in the presence of your children?

Read 2 Samuel 6:12-23. What do you think about a leaping and dancing king? Why was David's wife upset? What is the difference between David's heart and Michal's heart? How did David model unashamed public worship for us today?

Read Revelation 5:6-14. What are the different creatures in heaven? What are they celebrating? How is praising God described as a global event? How does seeing the praise of God by different species in this vision ignite our worship?

## Disciple

Let's get practical. What is praising and singing to God like for you every day? When do you set apart time in his Word? When do you listen to the Holy Spirit? Disciples of Jesus are able to praise God on their own without a worship leader or professional praise band. How do you praise the Lord alone? When does your family praise God together?

## Dedicate

Father, thank you for creating us for worship. We confess our struggle to praise you throughout the week. Please teach us how to praise you every day. We ask you to raise up our generation to praise you all the way to the ends of the earth, in Jesus' name and for his glory we pray, amen.

# Salvation Freedom
Romans 8:1-17

## Discover

Salvation is God's gift to the world. Jesus Christ died on the cross to rescue the human race. Freedom is the right to act and speak as we desire without resistance or persecution.

The truth is the most important pursuit of our lives: to search the world for answers to why we exist, what our purpose is, and what the future holds. The gospel of Jesus Christ as Son of God, Savior of the World, and King of Eternity provides the unshakeable foundation for everything we believe and every decision we make. (Colossians 1:15-17)

Our Father desires everyone to be delivered out of slavery to the troubles of this corrupted world and adopted into his family as heirs to his divine kingdom. (Romans 8:15-17)

We are all like the lost son who wanted to enjoy his life far away from home. He lost everything. (Luke 15:11-14)

Jesus is the faithful Son we must become. While we wander in darkness lost and confused, God sent his Son to rescue the nations. He opened up a righteous pathway for anyone who believes to live by faith in his Messiah. (Hebrews 5:7-9)

The gospel message is an invitation to the most significant decision anyone will ever make: to drink deeply from this Salvation Fountain, singing his praises, for we are restored back to a relationship with our Creator. (Isaiah 12:3-4)

This lesson provides a foundation for our discipleship mission. Our salvation and eternal life are grounded in what God did through Jesus Christ, not what we do to practice being good people. This teaching sets our aim on knowing, experiencing, and depending upon Jesus for everything.

# SALVATION FREEDOM

## ROMANS 8:1-17

# Draw

Father's heart: circle & heart - God's heart is for everyone he creates to become his sons and daughters: praising his holy name and enjoying our relationship with him. God loves the world, and we call him "Abba Father." (8:14-15)

Rebellion: arrow & running man - Everyone turns from God and runs far away, choosing to live apart from his design and separated from his presence. God made us to worship him, but our flesh makes us live for ourselves. (8:7-8)

Bondage: circle, winding path, & arrows - When we wander away from God, we become broken. We fall into bondage: living in spiritual darkness and blind to the truth. Our flesh is our rebellious nature. We reject God's commands. (8:12-13)

Surrender: arrow & praying man - When we learn about Jesus, we discover his call to turn from rebellion, surrender to him as Lord, and receive his forgiveness. When we surrender to Jesus, we die to our old lives and are reborn into his resurrection life. His life lives within us. Jesus saves! His life grows in us as we spend time with him. (8:10-11)

Jesus & the Holy Spirit: circle, arrows, cross, crown, & flame - Our Father sent Jesus to die as the perfect cure for our rebellion. His resurrection from the dead proves that he is the Son of God. Jesus received all authority in heaven and earth as Heaven's Salvation Door for all who believe. The Old Covenant Law of Moses required death and sacrifice for forgiveness; Jesus' death was the final sacrifice. (8:3-4)

Restored: arrow & praising man - As God's adopted sons and daughters, we are now eternal coheirs with Christ. We sing his praises and enjoy his presence. We were under condemnation because of our rebellion; now, we are alive and free in Christ through the Holy Spirit. (8:1-2,16-17)

## Discuss

Romans 8:4 mentions a "righteous requirement" necessary to live God's way. What is this righteous requirement, and why is Jesus the only one able to fulfill it?

Take a closer look at Romans 8:5-11. Why do you think we still rebel against God sometimes rather than walk in the Spirit? What are some signs that we are wandering away from God even after we have decided to follow Jesus?

When you pray, do you call God "Father?" Why or why not? According to Romans 8:15-16, if you do not speak to God as Father, do you think you should? How does the picture of a good father transform our daily relationship with God?

We see one clear purpose in 1 Peter 2:9-10 for why Jesus saves us. What is this purpose? Are you participating in this mission? If so, how? If not, what is one next step you can take towards living out this purpose personally?

## Disciple

Let's get practical. Romans 8:15 reveals the daily struggle between slavery and sonship, fear and courage. Whom do you know that wrestles with some clear type of spiritual bondage? What is one simple next step you can take this week to guide your friend closer to salvation freedom?

## Dedicate

Heavenly Father, thank you so much for adopting us as beloved sons and daughters through Jesus' death and resurrection. Please help us embrace your truth that we are now free forever from all condemnation. Please give us eyes to see people we know in need of freedom, and the faith and courage to reach out to them with compassion and peace, in Jesus' name and for his glory we pray, amen!

# Resurrection Identity
1 Peter 1:1-25

## Discover

Resurrection means raising someone from the dead. Identity is the knowledge of what we are, our existence.

God sent Jesus to redeem us, so that we will become his sons and daughters. He sends the Holy Spirit to live within our hearts, so that we are able to participate in God's affection for us. We call God "Father." (Galatians 4:4-7)

We are new creations in Jesus. God claims victory over our rebellion through Jesus' death and adopts us into his family through Jesus' resurrection. (2 Corinthians 5:17-19)

The Holy Spirit showed the prophet Ezekiel a vision of a valley filled with dry bones. When the Holy Spirit breathed upon the bones, they became living people. Only after their resurrection did they know God's identity. (Ezekiel 37:1-6)

Resurrection changes everything. Peter said we used to be scattered individuals, and now we are a unified people. We used to be lost in darkness, and now we live in marvelous light. We used to be wicked rebels; now, we are a chosen race, a royal priesthood, and a holy nation. (1 Peter 2:9-10)

Jesus taught Nicodemus, a Jewish ruler, about spiritual rebirth. No one can enter the kingdom of God unless they are born again. We must die to the flesh in order to receive a new birth in the Holy Spirit. The kingdom of God is an unpredictable adventure with the Holy Spirit. (John 3:3-8)

This lesson will help us build the foundation for our faith upon the Rock of Jesus Christ; our identity is in his resurrection life. If we build our lives and families on anything else, we crumble and fall away. (Matthew 7:24-29)

# RESURRECTION IDENTITY

## 1 PETER 1:1-25

# Draw

Born Again: fruitful plant - Our Father has given a new birth to our dead spirits through Jesus Christ's saving power. He demonstrates mercy through our living hope grounded in Jesus' resurrection from the dead and eternal life. (1:3)

Son/Daughter: king & children - We are God's adopted children. We overcome the evil desires of our flesh by the power of his Holy Spirit. God is our Beloved Father, and he calls us "sons and daughters." (1:14)

Faithful Friend: Jesus & disciple - We love and believe in Jesus. This faithful friendship with him bears a spiritual harvest of overwhelming joy. Jesus has proven that we can trust him and invite others into a friendship with him. (1:8)

Kingdom Heir: shining crown - We are coheirs with Christ. Our Lord Jesus keeps our inheritance with him in heaven until Judgement Day. Our salvation is secure; we are hidden in Christ and protected by his power through faith. (1:4-5)

Battle-Ready Warrior: sword & shield - We are warriors who maintain hopeful, alert, and sober minds. We are prepared for attacks of the enemy and desire our King's return. Our confidence is in our Lord Jesus' extraordinary grace. (1:13)

Holy Priest: anointing oil - Jesus is our Healer and Deliverer. As we practice holiness, his power and grace overflow through our lives into those around us. We want to be like our Savior Jesus who is righteous, merciful, kind, noble, excellent, marvelous, courageous, pure, and just. (1:15-16)

Anointed Ambassador: bridge over river - Jesus is our Master of Sorrows and Messiah King of Glory. He sovereignly scatters us throughout the earth to reveal our Father's glory through his Son by the power of his Holy Spirit. We are set apart to participate in his mission. (1:1-2)

## Discuss

Read 1 Peter 1:5-7. Refining is a process that removes impurities from a substance. How do trials and suffering refine our faith? Why does genuine faith tested by suffering result in greater praise of God? How are you suffering?

Read Galatians 2:19-21. How is our new birth in Christ described? How is it possible for Jesus' life to live within us? Why can we never be completely obedient to the law?

Read Philippians 2:13-18. How are faith, perseverance, and joy related to being children of God? What are some ways the culture of this world opposes faith and trust in God? What are some challenges to remaining faithful in this life?

Read Romans 6:8-11. We have not only died and been reborn, we also have victory over the power of evil. How did the devil control you before you became Jesus' disciple? What have you learned about your new life?

## Disciple

Let's get practical. Look back through these seven identity statements about disciples. Which ones are you living out? Which ones are new? Take some time alone or in your gathering to pray through these identities. Embrace each one, praise God for what he has done, and pray for boldness to share these resurrection identities with others.

## Dedicate

Father, thank you for being our Sovereign Creator, Compassionate Father, Trustworthy Companion, Messiah King, Master Commander, Generous Provider, and Almighty God. Please help us see ourselves in Christ the way you do. Please help us share with others these resurrection life identities, in Jesus' name and for his glory we pray, amen.

# Fruitful Vineyard
John 15:1-17

## Discover

Fruitful means a healthy plant or tree producing an abundant crop of delicious fruit. A vineyard is a field planted with grape vines producing grapes for making new wine.

Our Father set apart man from everything he made, creating only humans in his image. He planted Adam and Eve in Eden Garden to tend the vegetation and give special names to every being. He created Eve from Adam's body: another branch to display his majesty. (Genesis 2:15-22)

Abundant life flourishes wherever living water flows. Our Father can transform deserts and dry lands into harvest fields and vineyard plantations that sustain growing communities. Vineyards are a blessing. (Psalms 107:35-38)

Solomon wrote a song about Jesus, prophesying about the future Messiah's prosperous kingdom. His dominion is like a fresh rainfall of flawless justice: adopting orphans, caring for widows, and defending the poor. (Psalms 72:1-7)

Vineyards produce grapes which people eat as fruit or preserve for later. Grapes are also used to make wine. Jesus compared the Holy Spirit to new wine and our traditions to old wine. We cannot become comfortable in our old ways; so, we desire daily to be new. (Luke 5:37-39)

This lesson is about our role and position in God's kingdom. We are his branches; we are living water channels. Isaiah prophesied about heaven. One day, there will be no more miscarriages or premature deaths, no more war or worry, no more crime or curses. We will live with our Loving Father forever, experiencing his perfect blessings and abundant generosity as families and communities. (Isaiah 65:20-23)

# FRUITFUL VINEYARD

# JOHN 15:1-17

# Draw

Family Vineyard: vinekeeper & vine - Jesus' Church is like a fruitful vineyard. Our Father is the vinekeeper, Jesus is the vine, the Holy Spirit is the living water, and we are the branches. We share in God's work to cultivate crops. (15:1-2)

Living Water: vine, branches, & fruit - Branches die when they dry up; the living water flows through the branches to produce fruit. Jesus has designed us to remain in him, so that he will produce a bountiful harvest through us. (15:4-5)

Captured Heart: heart & crown - Jesus captures our hearts for his kingdom and glory. Faithful communion with our King aligns our desires with his, so that our obedience to his commands flow from our praises, prayers, and faith. (15:7-9)

Pruning Process: branches & fire - Our Father prunes our values. He loves us enough to cut off every poisoned branch of our lives, so that we become true disciples. We welcome his refining fire to purify and cleanse us. (15:6)

Perfect Joy: well & fountain - We experience unity with and affection from our Compassionate Father through Jesus' peace. Joy overflows like a living water fountain out of this eternal well of Christ's love. We gladly obey him. (15:10-11)

Pure Love: crucified messiah - Jesus demonstrates the perfect, sacrificial love of God's kingdom by laying down his life as the final payment that completely covers mankind's rebellion debt. It is finished! Jesus calls us "friends," because we participate in our Master's mission. (15:12-13)

Enduring Fruit: fruit bowl - Jesus sovereignly chooses each of his disciples and commissions us to live fruitful lives. The fruits of this earth spoil, but the spiritual fruit and gifts of Jesus' kingdom never die. His fruit includes love, friendship, faith, trust, power, confidence, and empathy. (15:15-17)

## Discuss

Read John 15:5-8. Our God is the Gardener, and we see a picture of him pruning healthy branches and cutting off dead branches. What is it like to be a dead branch? Share a recent experience of how God has pruned you for growth.

Read John 15:12-17. Why is the greatest love in the universe laying down your life for a friend? What are some differences between a slave and a son? What is the relationship between loving each other and producing fruit?

Read Psalms 62:5-8. This lesson is focused on teaching total dependence upon God for everything. Discuss God's names in this passage: Hope Source, Rock, Salvation, Fortress, and Refuge. How do these names ignite a passion in our hearts to personally depend completely upon him?

Read 1 Corinthians 3:6-9. Both John 15 and 1 Corinthians 3 testify that God alone produces fruit. We cannot be fruitful unless we abide in him. Are you depending on anything else? How does this knowledge humble us in serving him?

## Disciple

Let's get practical. Let us make sure that we fully embrace Jesus' teaching about abiding in him. What are some challenges to remaining in Jesus all the time? Consider your weekly activities; how can you practice God's presence at home, at work, as you travel, as you entertain? Ask God for help. Begin praising and praying more throughout each day.

## Dedicate

Father, thank you for this beautiful story of how we are connected to you and interconnected with other disciples. Please help us to abide in you, to practice your presence every day, in Jesus' name and for his glory we pray, amen.

# Journey Navigator
John 15:26-16:15

## Discover

A journey is the course of travel towards a particular destination for a specific purpose. A navigator is a person who guides someone or a group along an expedition.

Jesus said that he and the Father will make their home inside each person who loves and follows him. God lives within us when we believe in Jesus and repent of evil. He sends the Holy Spirit to live in us, teach us everything we need to know, and give us relieving peace. (John 14:16-27)

After Jesus' resurrection, he visited his disciples and spoke peace over them. He commissioned them to share the good news with all the nations; then, he breathed upon them so they would receive the Holy Spirit. (John 20:19-23)

Isaiah describes the Holy Spirit as our Teaching Companion. He teaches us how to walk along righteous paths and discern God's directions. He comforts us through mourning and assists us in identifying our idols. (Isaiah 30:19-22)

Paul says the Holy Spirit's presence provides freedom. We must confess that we are slaves to evil and turn to the Lord. Then, he destroys our bondage and unveils his glory. We only see God clearly through the Holy Spirit, who shepherds us to be more like Jesus. (2 Corinthians 3:16-18)

This lesson teaches us to listen to the Holy Spirit. He is with us: one of God's greatest gifts to creation. The Holy Spirit is our greatest resource on earth. He is God with us, and he always speaks into our hearts and minds what the Father and Son are saying. We do not have to worry about how to witness to others, because the Holy Spirit will teach us what to say each moment as we listen to him. (Matthew 10:19-20)

# JOURNEY NAVIGATOR

## JOHN 15:26-16:15

# Draw

Truth Advocate: flame, cloud, & crown - The Holy Spirit is like a fire from heaven speaking the revelations of God the Father and God the Son to us. An advocate is a spokesperson for someone else. The Spirit testifies to us, and then we turn around and testify to others. (15:26-27)

Persecution Prophecy: disciple, cross, & road - Jesus prophesied that his disciples will face great persecution for following him. Persecution is a test of our faith. When we face condemnation and pain, we struggle to endure. (16:1-4)

Grieving Heart: broken heart & tears - Imagine what it must have been like for the disciples who were with Jesus to realize he would leave them. Their hearts were broken, and their eyes shed many tears over his departure. (16:5-6)

Heaven Doorway: open door & sunrise - Jesus had to ascend back to heaven. He is the incarnate Son of God. He lives in his resurrected body and cannot be everywhere. He ascended to send the Holy Spirit to live within us and speak God's revelations to us, so that we will know his will. (16:7-8)

Eternal Pathways: disciple, paths, serpent, & Jesus - The Holy Spirit serves God in very specific roles: being present within us, convicting our hearts of evil, training us in holy living, and teaching disciples about spiritual realms, angels and demons, and the approach of Judgement Day. (16:8-11)

Wonderful Counselor: archer, arrow, & target - We cannot handle all of Jesus' revelations at once, so the Holy Spirit helps us focus on specific truths. The Holy Spirit counsels us in Jesus' will and unveils glimpses of the future. (16:12-13)

Trinity Champion: flame, heart, & crown - The Holy Spirit is a faithful servant to the Father and Son; he brings them glory and passes along to us whatever he receives. (16:14-15)

## Discuss

Read John 16:1-4. Why does Jesus teach about the Holy Spirit's work in the context of persecution and suffering? How can we include persecution and suffering as a natural part of the gospel message when we share with others?

Read Matthew 3:11-17. How does John the Baptizer describe the Holy Spirit? Why does John hesitate to baptize Jesus? How does Jesus' baptism story clearly reveal the Father, Son, and Holy Spirit? How does Jesus bring our Father joy?

Read Acts 16:6-15. How do we witness the Holy Spirit's work in this story? Have you ever experienced the Holy Spirit trying to stop you from doing something? What happened? How was the Holy Spirit preparing Lydia for salvation?

Read Revelation 3:20-22. How do we listen to the Holy Spirit? What does the Holy Spirit's voice sound like to you? How do we experience fellowship with God through the Spirit? What is the Holy Spirit saying to your church today?

## Disciple

Let's get practical. The Bible uses specific words to explain how to hear the Holy Spirit: be still, listen, hear, discern, understand, and receive. What environment do you need to listen to the Holy Spirit? How can you discern between the voice of God, your own thoughts, and the devil's temptations? Take five minutes now to pray and listen.

## Dedicate

Father, we want to hear your voice and understand your will. Thank you for sending Jesus to rescue us out of death. Thank you for sending your Holy Spirit to live in us and speak to us. We quiet our hearts now and open up the door to hear you, in Jesus' name and for his glory we pray, amen.

# Kingdom Prayer
## Matthew 6:5-15

## Discover

A kingdom is a territory, and the people who live there are ruled by and under the control of a supreme king. Prayer is a conversation with God where we listen and speak to him.

David said that prayer is a refuge for the righteous. Wherever we are and no matter what is happening in our lives or going on around us, we are free to look to God and speak, examine our hearts for any evil and rebellion, seek forgiveness and healing, and ask for help. (Psalms 5:1-7)

Elijah wanted to die. He was afraid for his life, because a satanic queen threatened to kill him. He ran into the wilderness and prayed for death. God sent his angel to bring him fresh baked bread and revitalizing water so he could recover and travel to a safe place. (1 Kings 19:2-9)

Jesus' strategy for preparing to be tortured, crucified, and die was prayer. He took his disciples to a garden and spent time with the Father pouring out his heart, grieving so deeply that his sweat became blood, confessing his weaknesses, and affirming his willing heart. (Luke 22:39-45)

James said praising and praying are the two greatest activities for all disciples. Is everything going well for you right now? Then praise the Lord! Is everything falling apart? Now is the time to pause and pray. We confess any evil in our hearts and invite our Lord to work in us. (James 5:13-18)

This lesson will focus our journey with God upon prayer. This age is temporary. We are preparing for the next age where disciples from every nation, tribe, people, and language together with all the angels will gather around Jesus' throne to praise him forever. (Revelation 7:9-17)

# KINGDOM PRAYER

## MATTHEW 6:5-15

# Draw

Humble Prayer: kneeling prayer warrior - Prayer begins with a deep love for and desire to spend time with our Father. Prayer is a conversation with God within the context of a close relationship with him. God already knows all of our needs and everything we will say before we speak. (6:5-8)

Awesome Wonder: father & children - Praise God! Glory, glory, hallelujah! So often when we pray, our first words are about ourselves and our needs. Let us begin our prayers in awesome wonder of God's majesty and glory. (6:8-9)

Advancing Dominion: crown, cloud, & earth - We align our prayers with what our Father wants: his kingdom to advance into the hearts of everyone who does not believe in him and for all peoples to seek and fulfill his will. (6:10)

Promised Provision: food & drink - Our Father cares about our daily living needs and invites us to ask for provision. We trust him to take care of us, provide for and protect us, and supply generously out of heaven's storehouses. (6:11)

Forgiveness Culture: divided people - God forgives. He initiates forgiveness in conflict. If we are true disciples, how can God bless us if we withhold forgiveness from others? Let us search our hearts for unforgiveness. (6:12,14-15)

Evil Enemy: prisoner set free - Our spiritual growth takes place within spiritual warfare. Our enemy is a fallen angel that strives day and night to attack us with temptation to evil. We do not fight our enemies. We seek God alone, crying out to him for deliverance and safety. (6:13)

Powerful Glory: shining city - We are sojourners in this life; travelers on a spiritual journey towards heaven. Our eyes and thoughts are fixed upon Jesus Christ. We do what he does, say what he says, and desire what he desires. (6:9-10)

## Discuss

Read Matthew 6:9-13. Discuss Jesus' prayer. How is this prayer simple? How does this prayer address the felt needs of our hearts and the changing seasons of our lives? What do you notice about the prayer and why does it stand out?

Read Psalms 51:1-13. King David wrote this prayer after going to bed with his friend's wife, getting her pregnant, and then having her husband murdered. Why do we need to confess our evil to God? How does confession lead to restoration? How do you feel after confessing your failures?

Read Luke 18:9-14. What is wrong with the Pharisee's prayer? What do we learn about faith and humility in prayer? How do we practice humility with one another?

Read Acts 4:23-31. Why is prayer one of our greatest resources for Spirit-filled living? Why did the church pray for boldness? What role did the Holy Spirit fulfill in this story?

## Disciple

Let's get practical. We are so weak in wisdom and clueless about life without Jesus Christ. Prayer is the open door to receiving understanding and power for following our Messiah King. How can we pray alone more? When can we pray more with others? Why is it so difficult to pray all the time? Pause now to pray. Ask God for a prayerful lifestyle.

## Dedicate

Father, thank you for prayer. Thank you for sealing us with your Holy Spirit. Thank you for caring about us and listening to our prayers. Thank you for revealing your heart for a daily relationship with us. Holy Spirit, thank you for teaching us how to pray and what to say. We commit to pray always with faith, in Jesus' name and for his glory we pray, amen.

41

## Sabbath Rest
Hebrews 4:1-13

### Discover

Sabbath is a culture of restful living. We abide in Jesus through worship and prayer every day and night. Rest means to cease intentionally from labor to relax, refresh in the Lord's presence, and receive his vision for each day.

Our Father created us for relationship. Every day, he visited Adam and Eve in the garden during the cool of the evening to talk. The first sign that evil entered the heart of man was Adam and Eve hiding from God in shame. (Genesis 3:8-11)

God is the Creator of the Ends of the Earth. He is eternal, and he made everything. No one can comprehend his majesty, measure his power, or understand his wisdom. He gives us his strength as we grow weary. (Isaiah 40:28-29)

King David calls God our Rock, Salvation, Fortress, and Refuge. We build enduring faith on the rock foundation of Jesus' righteousness; by his stripes, we are healed. We are safe and secure in the arms of our Father. (Psalms 62:5-8)

We place our trust in God alone and depend completely upon his faithful care. He never sleeps, and he watches over us as we rest. He is a Protective Shade covering us during spiritual attacks, and he is always with us wherever we are. God is our Loyal Companion. (Psalms 121)

This lesson teaches us the wisdom of embracing God's rest. We easily lose track of the most important values of life. God's rest is a set apart sanctuary for us to visit and remember our identity and purpose. God's rest is the tree of life where the living water of Jesus flows and the fire of the Holy Spirit blazes brightly. Rest is our refuge: the treasure of heaven and storehouse of eternal life. (Proverbs 3:13-26)

# SABBATH REST

HEBREWS 4:1-13

# Draw

Restful Refuge: open door & river - Our Father has created a special refuge where his children may enter in and receive rest. God rests, and he delights in us when we share in his rest. This rest is crucial to our health. (4:1,9-10)

Creation Pattern: crown & stars - God made the universe, declared everything good, and set apart one day for rest. God designed this ancient pathway to enter his presence by faith and reorient our lives to his leadership. (4:2-4)

Hidden Blessing: cloud & sunrise - Many before us have rejected God's rest. His rest is always available; however, we have demonstrated a habit of refusing God's gift. We disobey our Master when we forsake his rest. (4:5-6)

Hard Hearts: crown, barrier, & heart - Each day, our Father speaks his invitation to our hearts to rest, but we tend to harden our hearts against his voice. This rest is available every moment through the Holy Spirit's presence. (4:6-7)

Dragon's Curse: serpent & crown - The dragon is a wicked angel who led a rebellion against heaven. God cast him into hell: an eternal place of suffering and punishment. The dragon can never rest, and those who choose not to enter God's rest reveal that they are under his curse. (4:5,8,11)

Special Sanctuary: bridge over water - We begin from a place of labor and exhaustion. The Holy Spirit helps us to see this sanctuary where we can rest. As we join our Father in resting from work, we experience his peace. (4:9-10)

Living Word: sword & heart - Jesus is the Word of God. He is a surgical sword that penetrates our souls and exposes our bondage to the idols of this world. He is our Loving Judge, shining his divine light so that we will embrace truth. We discover true rest when we remain in Jesus. (4:12-13)

## Discuss

Read Hebrews 4:9-13. What is so special about the rest of God? Why do we have to enter into his rest? What happens to us if we do not rest? What is the difference between leisure and the rest of God? What role does his Word fulfill?

Read Psalms 1:1-3. How do the riverbank trees illustrate disciples resting in God? Why is daily time in God's Word so essential to strengthening our faith? What is the relationship between drinking from Jesus' living water and bearing fruit?

Read Mark 1:32-39. Jesus often behaved certain ways that perplexed his disciples. Why did Jesus wake up early and go somewhere alone to pray? How does Jesus demonstrate rest? How do we witness Jesus choosing God's will over the expectations of people around him?

Read Matthew 11:25-30. How does Jesus describe the mystery of God? Why must we approach God every day in faith with no expectations? What does Jesus teach about God's rest? What must we do to receive Jesus' comfort?

## Disciple

Let's get practical. We all have different jobs, personalities, passions, and family roles. Our starting place is busyness and long lists of important tasks. What have you learned about rest? How is resting in Jesus the answer to being fruitful as his disciple? Take a look at your weekly calendar; when can you schedule more intentional rest in our Father?

## Dedicate

Father, we praise you for this glorious rest you have created for us to enjoy. We are tired and weary; we need your help to rest in a busy and distracted world. Please guide us into your rest, in Jesus' name and for his glory we pray, amen.

# Heaven River
Ezekiel 47:1-12

## Discover

Heaven is the spiritual realm where God lives; there is no evil, pain, conflict, or death. A river is a stream of water flowing into another body of water like a lake or an ocean.

Ezekiel saw a vision of the Holy Spirit moving as a river flowing from the throne room of God to fill the whole earth with living water and abundant blessings. Wherever the river flows, life flourishes in every season. (Ezekiel 47:9)

King David wrote a song about God as our Shepherd who leads us beside quiet waters. This Heaven River is a righteous pathway where we are refreshed in his presence as long as we do not wander away. (Psalms 23:1-3)

As fresh water is essential to life on earth, so is the living water of Jesus to the spiritual health and eternal life of every child of God. The Garden of Eden was watered by a flowing river, so that fruit could be produced in every season to sustain life and nourish the land. (Genesis 2:10-15)

A living water river will flow from the throne room of God through the streets of the New Jerusalem in heaven. The Holy Spirit will produce consistent waves of crops to sustain life forever in Jesus' coming kingdom. (Revelation 22:1-5)

We want to become like Jesus as we follow him. Jesus practiced continual rest in the Father through the Holy Spirit, enabling him to fulfill God's will. (John 14:10-12)

This lesson will introduce disciples to the role of the Holy Spirit as our Wonderful Counselor and Life Navigator. We will experience the fruitfulness of heaven overflowing through our lives as we journey with him wherever he goes.

# HEAVEN RIVER

## EZEKIEL 47:1-12

# Draw

Heaven's Throne Room: temple, sunrise, & streams - The Holy Spirit flows out of the Father and the Son. The temple faces east illustrating Jesus' return. Multiple streams flowing illustrates the Holy Spirit moving across all nations. (47:1-2)

Walking Deeper: Jesus, Ezekiel, & water - The river is both wide and deep illustrating how the Holy Spirit is available to all who desire him. He helps us experience the glory of God as we surrender more to his guidance. Our calling is to seek rest in the Holy Spirit and float wherever he flows. (47:3-5)

Riverbank Forest: river, man, & trees - Wherever the Holy Spirit goes, there are people of peace who drink the living water and become disciples. The prophet has now fully surrendered to the Holy Spirit and depends completely on the Lord: resting in Jesus and flowing by faith. (47:6-7)

Abundant Life: river, fish, fruit tee, & animal - God is the Creator of life and light. The Holy Spirit brings the resurrection life of Jesus wherever our Father directs him. Living water creates new life and produces fruit. (47:7-9)

Catching Fish: fisher, net, & fish - The fishers are disciples on mission engaging the nations with the gospel. The Holy Spirit is present and moving. Those nearby desire Jesus' peace message and become committed disciples. (47:10)

Rotten Water: swamp & stench - The river goes everywhere desiring to rescue everyone, but many people will reject the living water. They are like still water with a bad stench, because their minds are selfish and spiritually dead. (47:11)

Fresh Fruit: shining fruit & bowl - The fruit of earth spoils quickly after harvest, but God's fruit is always fresh because of his power. Our role as Jesus' disciples is inviting anyone not in his kingdom to see and taste his healing fruit. (47:12)

## Discuss

Read verses 3-6 again. This river is huge! Why does Jesus lead Ezekiel deeper into the river? How has your life changed as you have followed Jesus over many years?

Read verse 8 again. Why does the river flow into the Dead Sea? What is significant about the river transforming the foul sea into fresh water? Has this story revealed any places of your heart that need fresh water from the Holy Spirit?

Consider the differences between verses 11 and 12. Have you ever rejected the flow of the Holy Spirit in your life? In contrast, how does it feel to be a channel for blessing as the Holy Spirit moves through your life? Give an example.

Take a look at Matthew 11:28-30. Jesus promises to give comfort to anyone troubled in heart. How is this comfort related to Ezekiel 47? Describe a time when you were suffering and how it felt for Jesus to send relief your way.

## Disciple

Let's get practical. What is one next step we can take to practice the presence of God more this week? Is there anything preventing you from walking in the Holy Spirit? Confess to God any "foul water" in your life. Pray, and invite the Holy Spirit to fill you more with the life of Jesus. What is one specific way you can be a blessing to others this week?

## Dedicate

Father, thank you for teaching us about your Heaven River. We repent of any foul water in our lives. Please shine your light into the deepest places of our hearts. Expose the bad water, and pour fresh water inside to cleanse us. Please show us how to be a river of fresh water to everyone around us, in Jesus' name and for his glory we pray, amen.

# Fire House
Ephesians 4:1-16

## Discover

A fire is the heartfelt worship, passionate emotions, and joyful enthusiasm we experience while enjoying our God. A house is the local residence of a family or group of people.

God created us to flourish within a community of families called a nation. Our Father adopted Abraham thousands of years ago, taught him how to worship, and committed to bless him and all the families of the nations. (Genesis 12:1-9)

God met with Moses in the wilderness and commissioned him to rescue the nation of Israel out of slavery in Egypt. Our Father reaffirmed his covenant love for his people and delivered them into a beautiful inheritance. (Exodus 3:4-10)

Jesus explained to his disciples God's plan to build the Church as his new covenant nation. Jesus' Church is a spiritual fire house shining brightly with radical love for the nations and authority over hell's armies. (Matthew 16:13-19)

Peter describes the Church as Jesus' family. Jesus is our Cornerstone: a rock solid foundation. We are living stones, royal priests, and a holy nation with a mission to share the good news of Jesus' glory with all peoples. (1 Peter 2:4-10)

Paul describes the Church as a spiritual gift treasury. God directs the Holy Spirit in distributing and activating these gifts among us; he intentionally created diversity. Every gift is special, and we all practice humility. (1 Corinthians 12:4-11)

This lesson teaches us about God's passion for unity and diversity. We all belong to God, and the Holy Spirit is in charge of spiritual gifts. Our diversity is wonderful! Let us embrace God's design and love each other. (1 John 2:7-10)

# FIRE HOUSE

# EPHESIANS 4:1-16

## Draw

Holy Foundation: house, heart, crown, flame, & fragrance - Our Father is building us, his Church, into a spiritual house. Our foundation is complete unity with the Father, Son, and Holy Spirit. Our humility and worship are a fragrant offering that fills our households with his holy presence. (4:3-6,9-10)

Fruitful Fellowship: table & meal - Some of Jesus' disciples are gifted shepherds: focusing on patience, practicing peace, and protecting unity. Shepherds love to gather people together for meals and encouragement. (4:2-3,11)

Gospel Mission: door - Some of Jesus' disciples are gifted evangelists: speaking the truth in love and witnessing to anyone not in a church. Evangelists love to leave the house temporarily to invite the lost to become Jesus' family. (4:7-11)

Daily Death: water waves - Some of Jesus' disciples are gifted prophets: practicing the baptism of the Holy Spirit's power and ministering Jesus' blessings to everyone. Prophets love to praise God and pray constantly. (4:5-6,11)

Warfare Training: sword - Some of Jesus' disciples are gifted teachers: avidly studying God's Word, memorizing vast amounts of Scripture, and cultivating an expansive understanding of God's kingdom. Teachers love to discuss the Bible and assist others to grow in the truth. (4:11,13-15)

Frontier Vision: mountain - Some of Jesus' disciples are gifted apostles: researching places and peoples without the gospel, praying for spiritual breakthrough, and mobilizing the Church into our Lord's harvest fields. Apostles love to train disciples how to reach unengaged peoples. (4:1,11-13)

Fire House: houses, flames, & fragrance - Jesus' Church is balanced and powerful when all the gifts come together in unity, and teams take the gospel into new homes. (4:11-16)

## Discuss

Read Ephesians 4:11-15. What gifts out of these five do you identify with the most? Why do we need all the gifts? What happens if we do not embrace them all? How do these gifts work together to keep us safe from evil and false teaching?

Read Jeremiah 29:4-7. How does God want to establish his people and bless them in spiritually dark places? What will happen if Spirit-filled families begin to seek the peace, freedom, and prosperity of the places where we live?

Read Mark 1:29-34. Why did Jesus decide to demonstrate his power and authority over sickness and evil spirits in homes and small towns? What do we learn about how to respond when we find people sick or captive in bondage?

Read Acts 10:34-48. How did Peter spark a new fire house? What is the gift of the Holy Spirit? Why did they baptize this family immediately? How can we welcome and embrace the Holy Spirit as the living fire of God in our hearts and homes?

## Disciple

Let's get practical. Ephesians 4 illustrates the healthy family of God captivated by his love for all the nations. Is there anyone that I need to meet with and ask forgiveness? How can we pursue relationships with disciples involved in other churches? What are my gifts and passions; what do I love to do for Jesus? What is one next step we can take towards sharing meals and the gospel with our neighbors?

## Dedicate

Father, thank you for making your home within us. Thank you for tearing the veil and opening up a new, living way for us to experience you every day. Please light a fresh fire within us, in Jesus' name and for his glory we pray, amen.

# Redemptive Time
## Ecclesiastes 3:1-15

### Discover

Redemptive means acting to save someone from evil. Time is the continual progress of existence and events in the past, present, and future viewed as a whole.

God created mankind for redemptive relationships. He is present and actively at work within our daily lives. He created us in his image to live within changing seasons with an awareness of and instinct for eternity. (Ecclesiastes 3:11)

Time flows through cycles of seasons. God created the world for us to enjoy and designed us in his image for worship. God delights in us when we faithfully follow him and depend upon his guidance. (Ecclesiastes 3:12-14)

Our Father invites us to journey along ancient paths that he has carved throughout this age. These are righteous roads paved by Jesus' work on the cross. He modeled for us how to surrender daily to God's voice as we rest in and listen to him. We must battle our natural inclination to chart our own course through life without him. (Jeremiah 6:16)

Jesus calls us to a surrendered life. Our greatest joy this side of his Second Coming is taking up our crosses to follow him. Our bodies and minds resist this call to deny ourselves and forsake the flesh; yet, this path of holiness is the only road to eternal life in heaven. (Matthew 16:24-27)

This lesson will help us balance our time so the fullness of God's kingdom will be released through our lives. We are called to be living sacrifices: searching our Father's heart in prayer, seeking first his righteous kingdom, discerning his revelation about our purpose, and waging war against the corrupted patterns of this age's societies. (Romans 12:1-5)

# REDEMPTIVE TIME

# ECCLESIASTES 3:1-15

# Draw

Wellspring Worship: disciple, well, & fountain - Our core identity is worshipers of God. All of us are called to care diligently for our own hearts and faithfully cultivate a personal relationship with God. He is the Source of our love, faith, joy, hope, and peace. Let us praise him! (3:14)

Marriage Garden: husband & wife - Marriage is a lifelong covenant relationship of intentional love. Embracing and not embracing is a balance of resting alone and enjoying community. Scattering and gathering stones illustrates practicing peace and reconciling during conflict. (3:5)

Healthy Home: parents & children - We invest daily in our children, spending face time with them as they grow. They are planted in our home for a season, then off they go. (3:2)

Sabbath Rest: tree, river, & person - We live in a busy, distracted society, so we have to reclaim the rest of God. Searching and letting go is about prioritizing, and keeping and filtering illustrates our values and passions. (3:6)

Diligent Labor: tent & tool - Our Creator designed us to care for the world. We discover unique satisfaction in providing for our family's needs. Tearing and mending represents healing and rebuilding. Silence and speaking up is about discerning when and how to share truth with others. (3:7)

Caring Community: cross & gathered disciples - We thirst for identity inside a safe, secure community. Jesus' Church serves this purpose. We gather in small groups to confess our brokenness and build one another up in love. (3:3)

Sharing Jesus: sower, soil, & seeds - Jesus illustrated God's kingdom as seeds sown into fields and grown into a great harvest. This process requires enduring patience with highs and lows, tears and laughter, sadness and dancing. (3:4)

## Discuss

We see a significant view of our purpose in verses 12-13; we should rejoice and enjoy a good life. Describe a "good life." How does our society define the good life? How does Jesus describe the good, blessed life in Matthew 5:3-12?

This passage describes 28 different seasons where each season is paired with the opposite to represent the full scope of human existence. How is it helpful to see all these experiences in a list? Which one(s) stands out to you? Why?

We do not perceive our life as a whole; instead, we focus on what happens today. The prayer in Psalms 90:9-12 says life passes quickly. What does it mean to "number our days?" What do you desire to do that you have not done?

James 4:13-17 describes the conflict between my will and God's will. Jesus teaches us to seek first God's kingdom in Matthew 6:33. When do you take time to ask God to reveal his will? What can you do when the answers are unclear?

## Disciple

Let's get practical. Here is the list of how we use our time: worship, marriage, family, sabbath, work, church, missions. Where are your strengths? Where are your weaknesses? What is at least one priority where you need to spend more time? What is the Holy Spirit guiding you to do next? Pray.

## Dedicate

Father, thank you for revealing the brevity of our lives in the context of eternity. Thank you for creating us for worship. Holy Spirit, we invite you to examine our hearts and expose missing priorities on our schedules. We lay our calendars at your feet, Master Messiah. Lord, have your way with the rest of our time, in Jesus' name and for his glory we pray, amen.

# Restoration Anointing
Isaiah 61

## Discover

Restoration is the process of healing something sick or broken to its original condition. Anointing is the presence of spiritual gifts and power upon someone blessed by God.

Isaiah 61 illustrates the Holy Spirit's presence resting upon God's people, so that we may participate in his mission to restore all nations as his beloved sons and daughters.

When we believe in Jesus, the Holy Spirit comes to live within us, opening up unhindered access to our Lord Jesus in praise, prayer, affection, and obedience. (Romans 5:1-2)

Jesus read from Isaiah 61, saying his mission fulfilled this prophecy. Even though he was performing miracles in the Holy Spirit's power, he was rejected. We too must expect rejection and even condemnation from our own friends, neighbors, and even close family members. (Luke 4:16-30)

The Spirit of the Living God is our Faithful Companion. He guides us with Jesus' wisdom so that our lives shine with grace. This grace captures the hearts of those around us, creating a desire to enter his kingdom. (2 Corinthians 3:1-6)

God's anointing is awesome! Therefore, we must be careful to remain humble and compassionate. The devil tries to corrupt our hearts with pride. The Holy Spirit distributes gifts according to God's sovereign will. (1 Corinthians 12:7-11)

This lesson will help disciples understand the purpose of the indwelling Holy Spirit's presence. He guides us as ministers of freedom, so that we will have compassion on and care for all who have wandered away from God's love.

# RESTORATION ANOINTING

## ISAIAH 61

# Draw

King: throne & crown - The Holy Spirit carries the divine authority of God to empower and guide believers in completing his mission to restore all nations. His kingdom is the healing influence in every earthly kingdom. Our Father cultivates hearts that praise his name in every tribe. (61:1,11)

Savior: cross & empty tomb - The Holy Spirit ministers Jesus' salvation to our hearts, assisting us as we repent of our evil and receive eternal life. We praise and worship the Lord because of his holiness, majesty, and splendor. (61:10)

Baptizer: waves - We once lived in shame and walked in disgrace; now, we are baptized by the Holy Spirit into an unquenchable joy fueled by his flawless love. Our disgrace was complete, our wickedness led to total disaster; now, we have been immersed in a double portion of God's favor and blessing. Our hearts are new; we love to be with God. (61:7)

Healer: laying on hands - The Holy Spirit pours resurrection life into devastation and helps us to be healers of the brokenness and humiliation all around us. First, we identify devastation; then, we patiently nurture renewal. (61:4)

Deliverer: key - The Holy Spirit anoints us with clarity of purpose: to seek out prisoners oppressed by spiritual bondage, embrace them, declare hope, and liberate them. The key to deliverance is the Holy Spirit's power. (61:1)

Shepherd: rod & staff - The Holy Spirit helps us guide our friends from every nation to participate in this freedom mission, so we may enjoy the fruit together. God creates within our hearts a yearning for a global family. (61:5-6)

Teacher: fruitful plant - The Holy Spirit is our daily teacher. He helps us experience the presence of God, so that we will become spiritually mature through Jesus' wisdom. (61:3)

### Discuss

What is the difference between the "anointing" of the Holy Spirit upon us in Isaiah 61:1 and the "sealing" of the Holy Spirit within us in Ephesians 1:13-14? Why do we need both?

Consider Paul's teaching in 2 Corinthians 3:17-18. Freedom is found wherever the Holy Spirit is present, and the Spirit lives in us. How can we participate in this freedom that is always present with us wherever we are? How can we help others near us experience his presence and freedom?

Take a closer look at Isaiah 61:11. Why do you think God chose to illustrate his salvation mission to all nations with the analogy of cultivating a fruitful garden? What skills are needed to "cultivate" spiritual maturity in someone's life?

What is the connection between the Holy Spirit's anointing in Isaiah 61:1 and Jesus' final commission to the disciples in Acts 1:8 to wait for the Holy Spirit to come upon them? What is the relationship between God's power and mission? Is it possible to complete his mission without his power?

### Disciple

Let's get practical. Isaiah 61:1-3 lists at least five actions of an anointed disciple. Do you know anyone with a broken heart, someone still mourning a loss, someone captive to spiritual bondage? What is the Holy Spirit asking you to do?

### Dedicate

Heavenly Father, thank you for sending the Holy Spirit to rest upon us in power. We gladly receive whatever anointings and gifts you desire to give. Please open our eyes to perceive these gifts, and guide us to follow Jesus in the power of your Holy Spirit. Please help us to walk in your freedom, in Jesus' name and for his glory we pray, amen.

# Warfare Armor
## Ephesians 6:10-20

### Discover

Warfare is the state of conflict between people resulting in battles and bloodshed. Armor is the protective covering worn by warriors to shield their bodies during battle.

When we decide to follow Jesus, we enter into the frontlines of a spiritual war. Though many do not see spiritual realms or beings, they are real and actively influence our daily lives. The evil powers of darkness try to deceive and distract us from enduring in our faith. (6:12-13)

When Elisha and his servant were surrounded by an army of enemy forces, the servant despaired for his life. The Lord opened his eyes to see an even greater host of warrior angels in the spiritual realm sent from heaven to protect God's messengers from enemy attacks. (2 Kings 6:15-17)

Jesus took three disciples up the mountain, and our Father transfigured Jesus so the disciples could see what he looked like in the spiritual realm. He spoke with the awakened spirits of Moses and Elijah about the future plans and events of his coming eternal kingdom. (Luke 9:28-35)

So much of what we know and understand about heaven, hell, and other spiritual realms and beings originate from dreams, visions, and prophecies recorded in Bible books like Isaiah, Ezekiel, Daniel, Jude, and Revelation.

This lesson exposes the spiritual war that has been raging in the heavens since the dragon led a demonic rebellion against God in millennia past. Discover the spiritual armor and weapons Jesus Christ created for his disciples, so we will stand strong and protected as we persevere in our faith through suffering and persecution. (2 Corinthians 10:3-5)

# WARFARE ARMOR

## EPHESIANS 6:10-20

# Draw

Spiritual Battlefield: cloud & swords - Our Father has designed gifts of spiritual armor for us to wear and weapons to wield, so we can stand in his power amidst ongoing spiritual battles against satanic enemies. (6:10-13)

Faith Shield: shield - We take up the shield of faith to stop the enemy's fire arrows from reaching us. The dragon's flaming arrows are designed to embed lies of the enemy within us, causing pride, fear, doubt, and despair. (6:16)

Salvation Helmet: helmet - We put on this helmet to guard our minds and remember essential truths: we have received salvation, we have died in Christ, and we are new creatures free from shame and secure in our God's strong arms. (6:17)

Truth Belt: belt - We buckle up the belt to stand firm against the enemy's lies and temptations. This belt holds everything together in his truth, so that we can identify and expose lies and accusations of the enemy. We reject whatever is false and embrace whatever is true and pure in Christ. (6:14)

Peace Sandals: foot & sandal - We put on these sandals, for we are peacemakers. We first believe and practice the gospel ourselves, then this peace overflows to others. (6:15)

Spirit Sword: sword - We take up the Word of God, the Bible, as a spiritual sword. His truth defeats the devil's lies. His truth cuts through the confusion and condemnation of the evil one so the lost can see Jesus and believe. (6:17)

Righteous Breastplate: breastplate - We put on the breastplate to cover our hearts where we believe and love. The dragon wages war day and night against the purity of our love and the steadfastness of our hope. God covers our hearts with his holiness; he protects us with his grace. (6:14)

## Discuss

Ephesians 6:11 describes the devil's schemes to attack us. How have you personally experienced the devil's attacks in your life? Has he ever been successful in knocking you off your feet? If so, how did you get back up and keep going?

Ephesians 6:18 tells us to pray at all times in the Spirit. First Thessalonians 5:17 teaches us to pray continually. How is constant prayer possible? How do you struggle with praying throughout each day? What can we do to pray more often?

Hebrews 4:12-13 also mentions the Word sword of the Holy Spirit with another purpose. Compare the sword's description in both Ephesians 6:17 and Hebrews 4:12. Why do we need this sword, and how do we wield it correctly?

We see the essential purposes of God's Word in 2 Timothy 3:16-17. Imagine a fully armed soldier missing his sword. What happens when a warrior goes into battle without a sword? What is life like when we are not daily in the Word?

## Disciple

Let's get practical. Practice putting on the spiritual armor and weapons of God. Make a list of people the Holy Spirit wants you to begin praying for regularly. Whom do you know today that has not heard of Jesus' armor and weapons? What is the Holy Spirit leading you to do next?

## Dedicate

Father, thank you for opening our eyes to see the spiritual war waging all around us. Thank you for crafting armor and weapons for the battles we face, and thank you for fighting our battles as we rest in you. Please help us to faithfully put on this armor daily and pray at all times in your Holy Spirit, in Jesus' name and for his glory we pray, amen.

## Scout Strategy
Nehemiah 2

### Discover

Scout means to explore a new area and gather information. A strategy is a plan of action to achieve a set of goals.

Following Jesus begins with a broken heart. Our Father's heart is broken over his lost sheep. He is constantly at work in the lives of those who do not love him. Disciples reflect his passion for redemption. Before we explore mission fields and discuss strategic plans, we need to fall on our faces before the King of Glory in prayer. (Psalms 34:14-22)

Moses sent scouts into the Promised Land to explore and gather information on the inhabitants. They returned with news about the beauty and fruitfulness of the land as well as a spirit of fear about the fortified strongholds. Joshua and Caleb tried to inspire the people to have courage and enter into the land by faith; however, Israel rejected God's commands and rebelled against his will. (Numbers 13:17-33)

Jeremiah prophesied about Israel's deliverance out of captivity to the Babylonian kingdom and return to God's kingdom. Sometimes God delays restoration to humble us. Waiting on God reveals our idols so we will turn to Jesus, praise his name, and receive healing. (Jeremiah 29:10-14)

Jeremiah also prophesied about Israel's glorious restoration: our wounds will be healed, our land will have peace, our rebellion will be forgiven, and all nations will behold our God's beauty and majesty! (Jeremiah 33:6-11)

This lesson teaches us to participate in God's mission to rescue the nations for his glory. Every disciple has the Holy Spirit within us for guidance each day. Identify those around you who will join us in Jesus' mission. (Hebrews 12:1-3)

# SCOUT STRATEGY

## NEHEMIAH 2

# Draw

Broken Heart: kneeling person - Nehemiah's heart was broken for his home city, which lay demolished in ruins. Sometimes the pain in our hearts is so intense that others can see the suffering inside reflected upon our faces. (2:1-3)

Restoration Vision: shining city - Our Father is on a mission to restore everything he has created. The Holy Spirit helps us to see visions of healing and restoration wherever we find brokenness. His visions inspire us to take action. (2:4-6)

Anticipate Needs: tree & axe - Nehemiah knew this restoration mission would be dangerous and require many resources. Our Father is a Wonderful Counselor who teaches us how to prepare for projects and missions. He is our Faithful Provider who supplies all that we need. (2:7-8)

Field Scouting: walking shepherd - Nehemiah went out alone during the night watch into his mission field to pray, listen to the Holy Spirit, and survey the environment where God had appointed him to rebuild the city. (2:11-15)

Team Mobilization: companions - Our Father designed us to flourish within a family and community. We need teammates to help us fulfill our calling. Nehemiah recruited resolute leaders and teams to help rebuild Jerusalem city. (2:16-18)

Persecution Preparation: cross & flame - We serve Jesus in the dangerous environment of an ongoing spiritual war. Wherever the gospel goes, we anticipate spiritual attacks, including persecution and suffering. The Holy Spirit helps us maintain faith, hope, and joy through many trials. (2:9-10)

Courageous Confidence: throne & crown - The devil will always attack Jesus' disciples when they advance his kingdom. Jesus has already claimed victory over the enemy, and we walk in his triumphant authority. (2:19-20)

## Discuss

Read Nehemiah 2:1-6. Share about a time when your heart was broken and someone noticed. Share about a time when you walked through suffering with someone else. How do brokenness and pain bring us closer together?

Read Acts 17:16-34. How did Paul and his team scout out Athens to discover their beliefs? How did Paul bridge from their views about God to the gospel? Why is learning about and listening to others' beliefs a good evangelism strategy?

Read 1 Peter 4:12-16. Why do you think our culture considers suffering people to be cursed? Share about a time when you experienced unbearable pain or an overwhelming challenge. How did you make it through?

Read Jude 1:17-23. What are some spiritual strongholds in our generation that have become barriers to people receiving eternal life? Why is there a warning to anticipate rejection from those we are reaching? How does Jude describe the Church as a Holy Spirit led mission team?

## Disciple

Let's get practical. Nehemiah demonstrates remarkable wisdom at each stage of God's mission to restore his people. How can we catch God's love for the lost around us? Whom do you know that still rejects his love today? What is the Holy Spirit revealing about one next step of faith you can take to reach them? Ask God right now to give you a loving heart for lost people and the courage to reach out.

## Dedicate

Father, you are Heaven's Missionary. Your love for the lost is too great for us to imagine. Please help us to love the lost as you do, in Jesus' name and for his glory we pray, amen.

# Disciple Craft
## Matthew 28:16-20

## Discover

A disciple is someone who follows Jesus: seeking the kingdom of God and walking in the Holy Spirit. A craft is the hands-on skills necessary to create a beautiful masterpiece.

Abraham's devotion to God was beyond any other disciple. He obeyed God's command to sacrifice his only son in worship. God was testing Abraham's faith and sent an angel to stop Abraham from slaying Isaac. God sealed Abraham's future family line with awesome blessings. (Genesis 22:9-18)

King David is a legend. He is renowned for being the disciple who ran after our Father's heart and danced in the crowded city streets, praising the Lord. His moral failures were devastating; yet, God chose to honor him and bring forth our Messiah through David's family. (Acts 13:21-23)

Elijah the prophet needed a successor, so God told him to find Elisha and anoint him. Elisha had no experience; he was a farmer. Elijah found him and brought him along as a companion to model faithful leadership. (1 Kings 19:16-21)

Jesus was brilliant at recruiting disciples. He created an environment where Peter and his companions could see God's kingdom for themselves. They listened to him teach, saw miracles, and left everything to follow him. (Luke 5:1-11)

Jesus was also deliberate in filtering his followers for truly dedicated disciples. He consistently challenged their resolve to absolutely trust and believe in him. (John 6:60-71)

This lesson is about discipleship: how to follow Jesus and invite others to join us on our worship adventure. We owe everything to Jesus who gives us life. (Romans 6:10-11)

# DISCIPLE CRAFT

# MATTHEW 28:16-20

# Draw

Faith Challenge: fishing pole & fish - When the disciples first met Jesus, he invited each one to follow him and learn how to fish for people. After Jesus' resurrection, he met with them again and challenged their faith. Was their faith authentic? Would they wholeheartedly follow him? (28:16-17)

Messianic Authority: Jesus & crown - Jesus has now received all authority in heaven and on earth from our Father. Jesus is the King of kings and Lord of Lords. He is the Great I AM. He deserves absolute allegiance. (28:18)

Discipleship Lifestyle: athlete - Discipleship is a lifestyle; we make disciples every day as we learn to walk with Jesus. We do not take time off from worshiping our Father. We do not take a vacation from our salvation. As we go throughout each day, we develop Jesus' kingdom light in others. (28:19)

Worldwide Vision: bridge over water - Jesus' Church is one global family with a focused vision for reaching every tribe, tongue, nation, and people with the good news. We love everyone, and we pray for the whole world to hear. (28:19)

Baptizer Culture: water waves - Every disciple has a destiny to become a baptizer by experience. In our culture, we have esteemed pastors as the only baptizers. God's Word teaches every disciple to baptize new disciples. (28:19)

Protective Guides: shepherd's rod & staff - Disciple makers are shepherds: soul guardians of new believers, healers of moral weakness, compassionate caregivers, dependable counselors, faithful companions, and loyal friends. (28:20)

Inextricable Immanuel: flame - Jesus' name is Immanuel, which means "God with us." You cannot remove the Holy Spirit from a disciple. You cannot extract salvation from Jesus' followers. His presence is a hope bonfire. (28:20)

## Discuss

Read Matthew 28:16-20. What does Jesus ask his disciples to do? What is a disciple? How do we make another disciple? Why do you think some of Jesus' disciples doubted him after seeing him alive? Do you have doubts?

Read Matthew 9:9-13. Why was it important for Jesus to share a meal with Matthew's friends at his house? Why were the local religious leaders upset? How does Jesus explain his vision for reaching the lost in our communities?

Read Mark 8:34-38. How do we deny ourselves? What are some examples of the competition between the world and the kingdom of God? What are some signs that someone is ashamed of Jesus? Why is it difficult to be Jesus' disciple?

Read Matthew 7:21-23. Jesus taught us to pray for help with obeying the will of God. How can we call Jesus "Lord" and not be his disciple? Why are miracles and spiritual power not proof that we belong to Jesus? What is God's will?

## Disciple

Let's get practical. Read Colossians 3:12-17. How do Jesus' disciples behave? How are we supposed to treat one another? How can we practice peace in the ways that we speak to one another? What have you done recently that you wish you could go back and change? What is one next step we can take this week towards Jesus' way of living?

## Dedicate

Father, thank you for inviting us to make disciples. Please help us praise your name, practice peace, speak with love, show compassion, forgive our enemies, and treasure wisdom. Holy Spirit, please show us whom you want us to disciple, in Jesus' name and for his glory we pray, amen.

## Prepared Receivers
John 4:1-42

### Discover

Prepared means to make something ready. A receiver is someone who opens up their mind, heart, and family to receive salvation from Jesus Christ, our Soul Rescuer.

The world was once doomed to annihilation by famine; however, God had been preparing Pharaoh to meet Joseph who would interpret his dreams. He also prepared Joseph to receive a worldwide deliverance plan. (Genesis 41:25-40)

King Nebuchadnezzar was a prideful, pagan king who sought only to exalt himself. The Holy Spirit humbled him by giving him the mind of a beast. Then, he repented and received a new heart to worship God alone. (Daniel 4:33-37)

God is preparing the nation of Israel to receive Jesus Christ as their Victorious Messiah. Though many Jews still reject Jesus today, the Bible is full of prophecies revealing clues about this Righteous King of Everlasting Light. (Isaiah 9:1-7)

Jesus prepared his disciples to expect his arrest, false trial, crucifixion, death, and resurrection. Peter resisted Jesus' prophesies, revealing his hard heart. (Matthew 16:21-23)

Jesus loved Peter, even though Peter denied knowing him three times during the night watch of his false trial. After his resurrection, he met with Peter, forgave him for the betrayal, and reestablished him as a faithful disciple. (John 21:15-19)

This lesson focuses on our hearts' condition. The Holy Spirit prepares us to hear and receive truth. We are unable to receive what God wants to give us, because we have dead hearts. We need Jesus to give us new hearts so that we will desire to follow wherever he leads. (Ezekiel 36:24-28)

# PREPARED RECEIVERS

## JOHN 4:1-42

# Draw

Spiritual Worship: praying person - Most people in the world grow up learning that worship is physical: go to a religious temple, give some money, and be a good person. Jesus teaches us to seek our Father with all our minds and hearts, and to worship him in the Holy Spirit and truth. (4:23-24)

Hidden Battles: cloud & swords - Everyone we meet is fighting hidden, personal battles. The woman Jesus met had experienced many broken relationships and was confused about who God is and how to worship. (4:16-22)

Intentional Compassion: road - The lost are outside in the world; we must go to places where we will meet them, just like Jesus did. Even though Jesus was tired, he loved this stranger and showed earnest compassion for her life. (4:1-9)

Thirsty Hearts: heart - Jesus knew exactly what to say to this woman to connect her thirsty heart with the gospel. The Holy Spirit helped Jesus communicate truth to this stranger in a way that cut through all her cultural and personal baggage to open her heart to receive God's love. (4:10-15)

Open Doors: open door - Once the woman discovered that Jesus was the answer to everything she had been searching for in worship, she went home and told everyone. She opened the door for them to meet Jesus too. (4:28-30)

Testifying Faith: fruitful plant - New faith in Jesus blossomed in this previously unengaged village because of the woman's faith-filled testimony. She was a prepared receiver: someone the Holy Spirit prepares for salvation. (4:39-42)

Harvest Season: wheat bundle - The kingdom of God is always flourishing with a great spiritual harvest. Jesus describes the different seasons of ministry, and how they all work together to produce glorious harvest crops. (4:31-38)

## Discuss

Read John 4:7-26. Jesus used one simple conversation to prepare this woman to enter his kingdom. How did Jesus engage her culture and beliefs? How did Jesus engage her heart? How did Jesus guide her patiently into the truth?

Read John 4:31-38. What food is Jesus talking about? What are the different stages of preparing for harvest season? Why is it hard to serve the Lord when you do not see any visible results? How does Jesus help us to persevere?

Read Isaiah 42:16. We discover a prophecy about Jesus as our Faithful Guide. Who are the blind, and why are they wandering in darkness? Why do we need God to guide us? How can these promises prepare a heart to believe?

Read Isaiah 62:10-12. Jesus creates clear paths for truth to be received where there were only closed doors and cold hearts before. How does God create clear paths in our minds to understand his will? Why do we need God to give us clear sight to see him? What happens when we see him?

## Disciple

Let's get practical. Think about the people you already know. Pray for them right now. Ask our Father to bless them, pour out his Holy Spirit upon them, and create clear paths of understanding for them to know him. Out of everyone you know, who is one person the Holy Spirit is prompting you to visit and guide them closer to Jesus?

## Dedicate

Father, thank you that Jesus is the Radiance of Heaven's Glory! Please help us to rest in your grace and shine your truth to all those around us. Please guide us to prepared receivers, in Jesus' name and for his glory we pray, amen.

# Peace Search
Luke 10:1-20

## Discover

Peace is freedom from hardship and struggle; a state of calming rest and sustained tranquility. Search means patiently trying to find something by careful investigation.

Jacob deeply hurt his brother Esau when he manipulated him out of his birthright and father's firstborn blessing. God had mercy on these brothers and prepared Esau's heart to forgive Jacob. These men practiced peace. (Genesis 33:1-11)

David was a mercenary before he became a king. He was constantly searching for safe places and people of peace who would help him escape from Saul's wrath. Abigail was a woman of peace married to a foolish man. Her wisdom, grace, and gentleness kept David from massacring her family. David eventually married Abigail. (1 Samuel 25:1-35)

King Solomon searched with all his might for peace. He built the most prosperous kingdom in history: developing urban infrastructures, innovating a futuristic society, and cultivating a global trade network. He wooed hundreds of royal women, pursued every pleasure available to a man, and researched the greatest depths of human knowledge. After all these accomplishments, Solomon had only one conclusion: life is worthless without God. (Ecclesiastes 2)

Saul the Disciple Persecutor had no peace. He tried to satisfy the burning rage in his heart by imprisoning innocent Christians, but he was never satisfied. Jesus showed up in a vision, blinded his eyes, rebuked his crusade, and gave him a new mission of making peace with all nations. (Acts 9:1-19)

This lesson focuses on peace. We need to know how to recognize Jesus' peace when we see it in the harvest fields.

# PEACE SEARCH

## LUKE 10:1-20

# Draw

Open Home: house & open door - When Jesus sent out the seventy two disciples on mission into villages, he taught them how to identify open homes. We will find people who desire Jesus and his righteous kingdom of peace. (10:5-7)

Harvest Prayer: praying disciples - Before we go out on mission, we pray for the fields. We ask our Harvest Lord to send out more workers. The Holy Spirit stokes a spiritual fire of love in our hearts for our lost neighbors' souls. (10:2)

Faith Mission: road over water - Jesus' mission is not easy. He describes his disciples as lambs among wolves. We depend upon his care and provision as we stay focused on him. We are not afraid of danger; we trust our King. (10:3-4)

Peace Invitation: disciple & flame - We search for people of peace who desire to receive the Holy Spirit and become God's children. Jesus promises to give us clear sight to see where his peace rests and where he is rejected. (10:5-6)

Intentional Fellowship: table, bread, & cup - Jesus teaches us to focus on one peace house. We cultivate friendship by sharing meals with the family and nurturing a trustworthy relationship. We are not called to invest our lives in people whom the Lord has not confirmed through prayer. (10:7-12)

Identify Bondage: disciple laying on hands - We identify sickness and pray for healing. We anticipate spiritual warfare and persecution. We engage people in love and faith, and then leave the results to the Holy Spirit. (10:9-17)

Kingdom Message: disciple speaking, crown, & listener - We disciple people in Jesus Christ's identity and stories. He alone has authority over the dragon. We teach disciples about his righteous kingdom and how to praise his name. Our focus is not on signs and wonders but faith. (10:16-20)

## Discuss

Read Luke 10:2-12. Review Jesus' instructions about advancing God's kingdom. What stands out to you about his strategy? Why do we need to go on mission with someone else? How do we know we have found peace?

Read Luke 10:13-20. How does Jesus describe the activity of spiritual beings in heavenly realms? What role does repentance fulfill in Jesus' gospel mission? Why does Jesus tell us to rejoice in our salvation rather than miracles?

Read Matthew 5:13-16. Jesus describes his disciples as salt of the earth and lights of the world. How does salt illustrate a disciple on mission? How does light illustrate a disciple on mission? Take a look at your light. How are you shining?

Read Jeremiah 6:13-19. What is the relationship between this passage and Luke 10:10-20. What is the difference between this world's peace and the kingdom of heaven? What do you think are the ancient paths of God? What are some signs that a person is rejecting Jesus and his peace?

## Disciple

Let's get practical. Where do you live? What are the names of local neighborhoods and marketplaces around your home? When is a good time on your weekly calendar to set aside for a prayer walk? Whom will you invite along for the adventure? Pray and ask the Holy Spirit for faith and favor.

## Dedicate

Father, thank you for opening up our eyes to see the harvest fields. Please give us a heart of compassion for our lost neighbors, a deep love for their souls, and a desire to visit them. Please guide us to the people you want us to engage, in Jesus' name and for his glory we pray, amen.

# Baptizer Mission
## Acts 10

## Discover

Baptizers are disciples of Jesus who engage lost people in their local communities, shepherd them into the kingdom of God, immerse them under water, and assist them as they practice the Holy Spirit's fruit and gifts. Our mission is to develop reproducing disciples worldwide in every tribe.

Jacob had a rough life and struggled to understand his purpose. One night, he wrestled with Jesus until daybreak and would not let go until he received a blessing. Jesus baptized Jacob into a new name and covenant identity: Israel, the Blessed Overcomer. (Genesis 32:22-32)

God baptized Moses in his glory. The seventy elders of Israel witnessed this awesome appearance of God's glory: pavement as bright blue as the sky, a brilliant cloud, and a consuming fire. Jesus first captures our hearts with his glory, and then he immerses us in his presence. Now that we are baptized in him, we walk daily with him. (Exodus 24)

Elijah was baptized directly into heaven. God sent angels in a fire chariot drawn by fire horses to pick up Elijah's physical body on earth and transport him to the spiritual realm of heaven. Jesus' baptisms create changes in both physical and spiritual realms of existence. (2 Kings 2:7-14)

When we experience God, we abandon the rebellion of this world. We receive pure joy and an eternal inheritance in the presence of Jesus. He never leaves us, and he navigates our steps safely through intense spiritual battles. Our responses are adoration and perseverance. (Psalms 16:5-11)

This lesson focuses on our experience of being immersed into the culture and convictions of Jesus' eternal dominion.

# BAPTIZER MISSION

## ACTS 10

# Draw

Anointed Adventures: disciples, flames, road, sunrise, & arrow - We are followers of Jesus Christ, anointed with the Holy Spirit's presence and power on an unpredictable mission adventure. Acts 10 tells a fascinating story about our Father tearing down strongholds of tradition, and pursuing unengaged families and tribes with the good news. Following Jesus is all about seeking his face and walking according to the directions of his Holy Spirit. Jesus honored Cornelius' sincere desires and faithful prayers, and sovereignly orchestrated his family's salvation. (10:1-9)

Covenant Household: house, flame, cloud, rainbow, & arrow - Jesus prepared Peter to encounter and engage a searching family with the gospel. Peter would not have gone to visit Cornelius without the vision and angelic visit. Our Father saw Cornelius' genuine thirst for his presence and kingdom, and revealed a vision that prepared Peter to embrace a new way of life. He confirmed his calling upon Peter to introduce this family to Jesus and assist them as they entered into a gospel covenant relationship. (10:9-34)

Resurrection Immersion: disciples, water, flame, wind, & arrow - Peter witnessed the spiritual hunger and thirst of Cornelius' family for Jesus. He preached the gospel of resurrection life to this family, and everyone believed. The Holy Spirit baptized them in power, and all of these new disciples began to participate in spiritual gifts and speak in spiritual languages. Peter baptized them in water and spent a few days teaching them how to follow Jesus. (10:35-48)

Calvary Calling: three crosses & hill - Peter had to put to death his religious traditions and personal interpretations. Cornelius took a leap of faith and invited a stranger from another culture over to his home. All the prophets, John the Baptizer, and Jesus Messiah call us to share in the suffering of Calvary where Jesus saved the world. (10:27-29,37-43)

## Discuss

Read Acts 10:1-16. Our Father prepared both Cornelius and Peter to meet each other. Why did God have mercy on Cornelius? How was Peter's vision perfectly tailored just for him? Why is God's direct intervention essential to this story?

Read Acts 10:34-43. How does Peter share the gospel with Cornelius' family? What details stand out to you? How do we see the Father, Son, and Holy Spirit clearly in this gospel proclamation? What is necessary to believe for salvation?

Read Acts 8:26-40. Make a list of everything supernatural in this story. What is the problem with this African royal court servant departing Jerusalem without any knowledge of Jesus Christ? How does Philip demonstrate a baptizer mission? Why does Philip baptize this new disciple at once?

Read Acts 19:1-7. How does someone receive the Holy Spirit? Can you believe in Jesus and not have the Holy Spirit? How do we see different baptisms in this story: salvation, water immersion, and the Holy Spirit's power?

## Disciple

Let's get practical. Review the Salvation Freedom lesson from Romans 8. Are you prepared to draw the gospel for someone and explain to them how to be saved? Where is the nearest location to your home where you can immerse a new disciple in water? Whom do you know that is lost but close to following Jesus? Pray for their faith and baptisms.

## Dedicate

Father, thank you for your baptisms and for inviting us into this baptizer mission. Please help us to truly embrace your authority and become experienced baptizers of new disciples, in Jesus' name and for his glory we pray, amen.

# Local Revolution
Acts 2:36-47

## Discover

Local means belonging or relating to a particular area or neighborhood. A revolution is the purposeful overthrow of a corrupt dominion or social order in favor of a new system.

The dragon used to be the most beautiful archangel in heaven. He was an anointed guardian cherub; a warrior angel who led the host of heaven in praising God. He saw the majesty, power, and perfection of his Creator, and his heart became envious. He attempted to overthrow God's rule and possess heaven for himself. God cursed him and cast him into hell: an eternal domain set apart for anyone who desires separation from God. (Ezekiel 28:11-19)

When our Father created Adam and Eve, the dragon visited them in Eden Garden. Despite God's love and a life in paradise, they decided together to reject him and follow the dragon. For this reason, we are all under the dominion of an abominable curse. Daily, we battle evil desires, the dragon's temptations, and a depraved world culture. (Genesis 3:1-19)

Our story does not end in despair. Jesus will return soon! His name is Faithful and True, his eyes are like blazing fire, and he wears many crowns representing his supreme command over every age past, present, and future. He will return to defeat the dragon's final assault on earth and heaven, seal him forever in hell, judge mankind, and usher in the next age where all things are new. (Revelation 19-21)

This lesson focuses on the Church as a new community on earth. We have been baptized into Christ; the old is gone and behold, the new is here. Together, we press into faith, hope, and love. We nurture a profound love for all peoples and coordinate plans to reach everyone. (1 Corinthians 13)

# LOCAL REVOLUTION

## ACTS 2:36-47

# Draw

Resurrection Covenant: water, disciples, & flames - Disciples baptized in water with the Holy Spirit resting upon them like a fire is a perfect picture of our new resurrection life in Jesus Christ. His life is now our life. We will never be the same after we surrender completely to his call. (2:36-41)

Jesus Focus: Jesus & light - Peter's message focused on Jesus: who he is, what he did, why he did it, and what it means for us. Peter also glorified Jesus' purpose, directing everyone's attention to his sacrifice and salvation. (2:36-39)

Breakthrough Prayer: kneeling disciple - When we enter this new life in Christ, we shift out of religious rites into an affectionate relationship with our Father. Jesus' Church prays all the time. We pray alone and together. Persistent prayer unleashes breakthrough in Jesus' mission. (2:42)

Legendary Generosity: shining & pouring cup - The first church was renowned for generosity. Everyone shared everything. Disciples met all the needs of those around them. They considered themselves one big family. (2:44-46)

Welcome Homes: houses & arrows - Jesus' Church desires to be together. We love each other, and we want to demonstrate that love however each of us are able. This church met together often, not just for worship gatherings, but also visiting each others' homes for fellowship. (2:46)

Communion Meals: table, bread, & cup - In the past, communion was a natural part of daily meals. Whenever the disciples met in homes for prayer and encouragement, they set apart time to reflect on Jesus' sacrificial death. (2:42,46)

Awakening Hearts: hearts & bridge - The result of Jesus' new church practicing a living gospel culture was a regional awakening: new disciples following Jesus every day. (2:47)

## Discuss

Read Acts 2:36-41. How do we see prepared receivers in this story? What did Peter teach is absolutely necessary for salvation? How do you repent of evil when you pray? What do you think it was like to baptize 3,000 people in one day?

Read Acts 2:42-47. Consider the churches in your community if there are any. Do any of them have a reputation like this church? What is missing from this story in your church? How can we become more like this church?

Read 2 Corinthians 3:17-18. The Holy Spirit is everywhere, and he is sealed in us. The Holy Spirit's presence creates freedom; therefore, every disciple of Jesus is a Freedom Bearer. How do we carry freedom? How can there be lesser and greater glory? How do we seek God's greater glory?

Read 2 Corinthians 12:1-10. We all grow tired and weary over time. No one is always victorious except Jesus. How do we practice grace? How do we embrace our weaknesses? How does Jesus fill our weaknesses with his powerful strength?

## Disciple

Let's get practical. What do you like about Jesus' first church? What is the Holy Spirit revealing in this story that you want to see happen in your church? What prevents our churches today from embracing this culture? How will we begin personally practicing the changes we want to see? Pray, and ask Jesus to fill our churches with fresh vision.

## Dedicate

Father, we want to be like your first church. We want your kingdom to come and your will to be done in our churches today. Please help us desire only you and invite others into your family, in Jesus' name and for his glory we pray, amen.

# Radical Culture
## Acts 2

## Discover

Radical means thoroughly affecting the fundamental nature of something. A culture is the beliefs, values, and practices of a people group connected through a united identity.

Israel's Commander Joshua led their army through a bold conquest of God's Promised Land. He gathered everyone together after they had settled in the region, and presented them different cultures to choose from. The leaders verbally reestablished their covenant promise to worship only Yahweh. Joshua prophesied that this culture would fail, because they would eventually rebel. (Joshua 24:14-28)

Joshua's prophecy came true; Israel rejected God. They lived among the nations, experienced other cultures and pagan gods, and chose to embrace the world. At this time in history, only the faithful kings and prophets could receive the Holy Spirit. Even though God's people witnessed waves of astonishing miracles, all these signs and wonders could not save them from their wicked, dead hearts. (1 Samuel 8)

Everything changed with the most well known birth of our age. God's Word clothed himself in flesh and bone, and became a man. Our Father breathed resurrection life over Mary, and she gave birth to Jesus Messiah: God with us, Savior of the World, Rescuer of Mankind, Banner for All Peoples, Prince of Peace, the Great I AM. He brought with him the gift of a marvelous culture that no one is able to understand or receive without the Holy Spirit. (Luke 2:1-35)

This lesson focuses on truths very difficult to express if you have not experienced God's love. Jesus makes all things new, transforming our desires and dreams. Now, all we really want is to praise Jesus and see his face. (Psalms 148)

# RADICAL CULTURE

## ACTS 2

# Draw

Zion Vision: heart, crown, flame, & light - Zion is the New Jerusalem. Heaven is the perfect city where we will live forever with our Father, Jesus Messiah, and the Holy Spirit. Our vision is to remain in his rest and promises. (2:29-36)

Adventurous Feet: road over water - Jesus' disciples welcome the Holy Spirit's guidance and counsel. He comes to live within us and shepherds us out of comfort, scattering us everywhere to invite all nations into his family. (2:1-12)

Open Invitation: table, bread, & cup - We keep the door open to salvation for everyone around us. Anyone who cries out to Jesus will be saved. Between now and when our Lord returns, we speak the truth in love as the Holy Spirit reveals whom to engage and what to say. (2:16-24)

Embrace Jesus: Jesus & disciple walking - Salvation is not the result of simply knowing the truth. Jesus tells us to deny ourselves, take up our cross, and follow him into suffering. We must fully surrender everything, and count the cost of participating in his kingdom as a faithful disciple. (2:36-41)

Storytelling Assemblies: houses, arrows, & cross - We are not disciples because we visit church services. The gospel must live in our hearts and homes; our hope is anchored in Christ. Jesus' Church is a Spirit-baptized, storytelling family. His stories come alive as our faith breathes. (2:25-32)

Guardian Shepherds: shepherd's rod & staff - Jesus suffered, and so will every one of his disciples. We need spiritual leader teams to cover all of our fellowships with prayer, wisdom, compassion, and teaching. (2:37-42)

Resurgence Waves: moving wave & water - God still moves. The Holy Spirit is waking up our cities and every nation. He gives dreams, visions, and revelations to everyone. (2:16-21)

## Discuss

Read Acts 2:1-13. How did the disciples experience God physically? How have you experienced God? What would it be like to speak in a language you do not know? Why did the Holy Spirit give the disciples gifts of many languages?

Read Acts 2:25-36. How did David prophesy about Jesus? Why was David not afraid of death? How does Jesus' revelation about God's eternal pathways fill our hearts with joy? Where is Jesus now? What is Jesus doing right now?

Read John 13:1-17. Why did Jesus wash his disciples' feet? Jesus washed the feet of his disciple who betrayed him. What does that mean? Have you ever blessed anyone this way by washing their feet? Whose feet can you wash soon?

Read Revelation 21. How does John's vision describe heaven? What do you notice about heaven's radical culture? What are some differences between our age and the age to come? How is God already dwelling with us?

## Disciple

Let's get practical. What are your most essential values? Does the way you spend your time reflect what you believe? Why or why not? Are you ready to stand before our Lord Jesus on Judgement Day? How can you begin to practice heaven's radical culture today? What are some questions you want to ask Jesus when you see his face?

## Dedicate

Father, thank you for inviting us into your radical dominion. We love you, Abba, and we are awestruck in your holy presence. For the rest of our days, we will live to enjoy your presence, praise your name, listen to your Spirit, and draw disciples, in Jesus' name and for his glory we pray, amen.

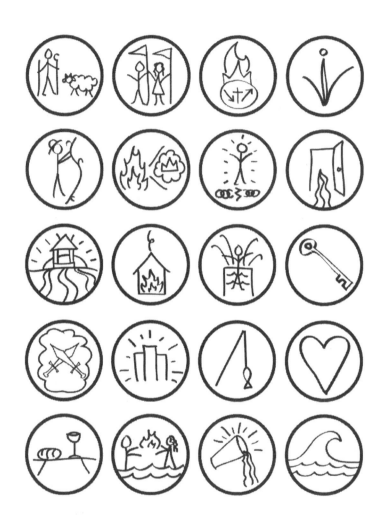

## Storytellers Game

A storyteller is someone who speaks stories to others.

Consider this recent news release from the International Orality Network (ION, orality.net):

"There are 4.35 billion people in our world who are oral learners. They are found in many cultural groups in the villages and in global cities around the world. We recognize that 60% of the world's population can't, won't, or don't hear the Gospel when we share it simply because it's often coming to them through literate means they don't understand and to which they do not relate."

We developed Draw Disciples in response to ION's Declaration of Action:

"We call upon the Body of Christ to devote energies, strategies, and resources to provide access for all oral learners to engage the entire Word of God through audio-digital means, so that every tribe, every tongue, and every people group may hear, understand, and have the opportunity to respond!"

**Are you up for our Storytellers Game Challenge?**

The following pages contain only the drawings for all 20 lessons in this book. Our fun memory game awaits!

Without looking back at the chapters, can you...

- Identify the stories and Bible chapters?
- Draw the stories without help?
- Use your drawings to tell the stories?
- Create your own drawings for each story?

Ready, set, go!

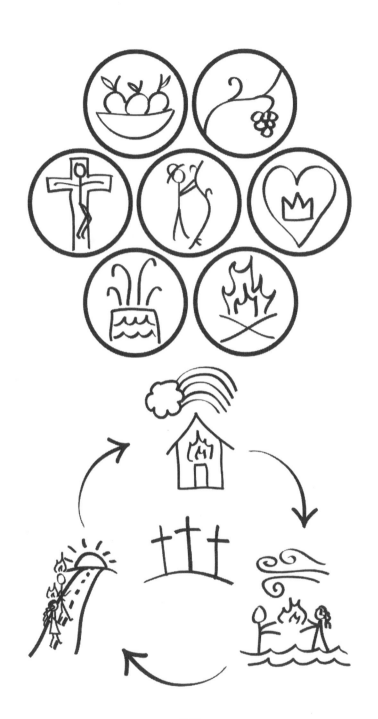

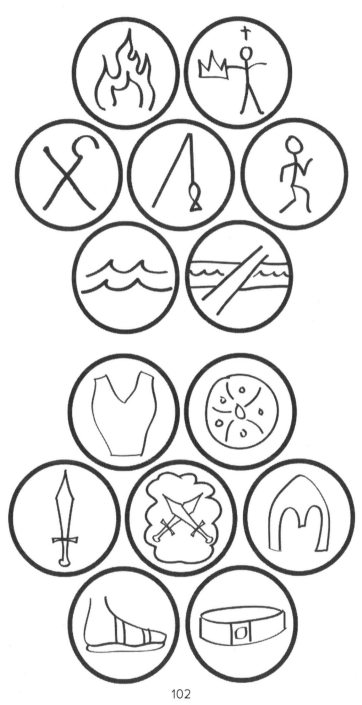

## Storytellers Book

We are excited to announce that we are now developing our next book, entitled "Storytellers."

Our vision is to create a resource that equips every disciple as a mobile storyteller ready to reach anyone, anywhere.

This epic storybook will have 600 Bible stories clustered into 50 story sets with simple sketches for easy storytelling.

Please enjoy the first 47 lessons we have finished!

## Yahweh Creates Everything Story
### Genesis 1:1 - 2:3

Sketch #1: God creating - This sketch is the story logo. Let me tell you a story about how Yahweh, Creator of Heaven and Earth, breathed out all creation.

Sketch #2: Mountain, birds, sea, and fish - This sketch illustrates the first part of the story where Yahweh creates the universe, lands, seas, and most creatures in the world.

Sketch #3: Tree, animal, and people - This sketch illustrates the second part of the story where Yahweh completes creation and commands mankind to be fruitful and multiply.

Sketch #4: God resting - This sketch illustrates the third part of the story where Yahweh declares all creation to be good, blesses mankind, and rests on the holy seventh day.

### Storyteller Discipleship

The following activities will help you remember the story, apply wisdom to your own life, and tell the story to others.

- Listen to the story. Draw the story.
- Tell the story with the drawings.
- Draw your own pictures to illustrate the story.
- Pray and ask the Holy Spirit to reveal wisdom in the story.
- What is the Holy Spirit asking you to do next?
- Draw a map of your family and friends and pray for them.
- Go and tell the story to someone. Discuss the story.
- Disciple others to become Spirit-filled storytellers.

**Mankind Rejects Yahweh Story**
Genesis 3:1-24

Sketch #1: Tree & fire sword - This sketch is the story logo. Let me tell you a story about the day we began to die.

Sketch #2: Snake & people - This sketch illustrates the first part of the story where Satan tempted Adam & Eve to rebel against God and become gods themselves.

Sketch #3: Eaten fruit - This sketch illustrates the second part of the story where Adam & Eve eat the fruit, discover they are naked, clothe themselves, and hide from God.

Sketch #4: Knife & animal sacrifice - This sketch illustrates the third part of the story where God cursed mankind. The first blood sacrifice was animal skins to clothe people.

### Storyteller Discipleship

The following activities will help you remember the story, apply wisdom to your own life, and tell the story to others.

- Listen to the story. Draw the story.
- Tell the story with the drawings.
- Draw your own pictures to illustrate the story.
- Pray and ask the Holy Spirit to reveal wisdom in the story.
- What is the Holy Spirit asking you to do next?
- Draw a map of your family and friends and pray for them.
- Go and tell the story to someone. Discuss the story.
- Disciple others to become Spirit-filled storytellers.

## Noah's Rainbow Covenant Story
### Genesis 8:1 - 9:17

Sketch #1: Cloud, rainbow, & boat - This sketch is the story logo. Let me tell you a story about the first rainbow.

Sketch #2: Dove & olive branch - This sketch illustrates the first part of the story where the flood is over, and Noah sends the birds out searching for dry land.

Sketch #3: Altar, lamb, & fire - This sketch illustrates the second part of the story where God commands Noah and his family to depart the ark, and Noah sacrifices an animal.

Sketch #4: Cloud & rainbow - This sketch illustrates the third part of the story where God establishes a new covenant with Noah. He will never destroy humanity again by flood and explains the meaning of the rainbow sign.

## Storyteller Discipleship

The following activities will help you remember the story, apply wisdom to your own life, and tell the story to others.

- Listen to the story. Draw the story.
- Tell the story with the drawings.
- Draw your own pictures to illustrate the story.
- Pray and ask the Holy Spirit to reveal wisdom in the story.
- What is the Holy Spirit asking you to do next?
- Draw a map of your family and friends and pray for them.
- Go and tell the story to someone. Discuss the story.
- Disciple others to become Spirit-filled storytellers.

## Babylon Tower City Story
### Genesis 11:1-9

Sketch #1: City & cloud - This sketch is the story logo. Let me tell you a story about why we have so many languages spoken throughout the world.

Sketch #2: Tent - This sketch illustrates the first part of the story where all mankind gathered together in one part of the world to build a massive city for one society.

Sketch #3: Man holds crown - This sketch illustrates the second part of the story where God saw man's idolatry to worship himself and walk in his own authority.

Sketch #4: Woman speaks - This sketch illustrates the third part of the story where God confused mankind by creating many tongues so they could not unite against him.

### Storyteller Discipleship

The following activities will help you remember the story, apply wisdom to your own life, and tell the story to others.

- Listen to the story. Draw the story.
- Tell the story with the drawings.
- Draw your own pictures to illustrate the story.
- Pray and ask the Holy Spirit to reveal wisdom in the story.
- What is the Holy Spirit asking you to do next?
- Draw a map of your family and friends and pray for them.
- Go and tell the story to someone. Discuss the story.
- Disciple others to become Spirit-filled storytellers.

## Joseph Slave Dreamer Story
### Genesis 37:1-36

Sketch #1: Man & pit - This sketch is the story logo. Let me tell you a story about 11 brothers who sold their brother who had dreams of the future into slavery.

Sketch #2: Cloak - This sketch illustrates the first part of the story where Israel favors Joseph and angers his brothers by giving him a multi-colored cloak of honor.

Sketch #3: Wheat & star - This sketch illustrates the second part of the story where Joseph had two dreams about his family bowing down to him.

Sketch #4: Knife & chain - This sketch illustrates the third part of the story where the brothers kill a goat to fake Joseph's death. Joseph travels to Egypt as a slave.

## Storyteller Discipleship

The following activities will help you remember the story, apply wisdom to your own life, and tell the story to others.

- Listen to the story. Draw the story.
- Tell the story with the drawings.
- Draw your own pictures to illustrate the story.
- Pray and ask the Holy Spirit to reveal wisdom in the story.
- What is the Holy Spirit asking you to do next?
- Draw a map of your family and friends and pray for them.
- Go and tell the story to someone. Discuss the story.
- Disciple others to become Spirit-filled storytellers.

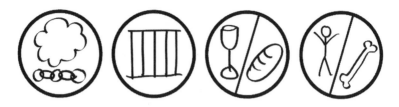

## Joseph Interprets Dreams Story
### Genesis 40:1-23

Sketch #1: Cloud & chains - This sketch is the story logo. Let me tell you a story about a dream interpreter in prison.

Sketch #2: Prison bars - This sketch illustrates the first part of the story where Joseph meets Pharaoh's servants in jail and takes care of them.

Sketch #3: Cup & bread - This sketch illustrates the second part of the story where Joseph listens to and interprets the two dreams about the future.

Sketch #4: Man & bone - This sketch illustrates the third part of the story where the dreams come true: the cupbearer lives and the baker dies. Joseph is forgotten.

## Storyteller Discipleship

The following activities will help you remember the story, apply wisdom to your own life, and tell the story to others.

- Listen to the story. Draw the story.
- Tell the story with the drawings.
- Draw your own pictures to illustrate the story.
- Pray and ask the Holy Spirit to reveal wisdom in the story.
- What is the Holy Spirit asking you to do next?
- Draw a map of your family and friends and pray for them.
- Go and tell the story to someone. Discuss the story.
- Disciple others to become Spirit-filled storytellers.

## Mount Sinai Covenant Story
Exodus 19:1-25

Sketch #1: Mountain & smoke - This sketch is the story logo. Let me tell you a story about how the nation of Israel saw God's glory come down upon a mountain in fire and smoke.

Sketch #2: Tent - This sketch illustrates the first part of the story where Israel arrives at Mount Sinai, sets up camp, and Moses receives covenant ceremony instructions.

Sketch #3: Water - This sketch illustrates the second part of the story where Moses helps the people purify themselves and prepare for God's arrival upon the mountain.

Sketch #4: Ram's horn blast - This sketch illustrates the third part of the story where God descended upon Mount Sinai and warns the people not to approach him yet.

## Storyteller Discipleship

The following activities will help you remember the story, apply wisdom to your own life, and tell the story to others.

• Listen to the story. Draw the story.
• Tell the story with the drawings.
• Draw your own pictures to illustrate the story.
• Pray and ask the Holy Spirit to reveal wisdom in the story.
• What is the Holy Spirit asking you to do next?
• Draw a map of your family and friends and pray for them.
• Go and tell the story to someone. Discuss the story.
• Disciple others to become Spirit-filled storytellers.

### Elijah's Fire Mountain Story
1 Kings 18:19-46

Sketch #1: Water & fire sacrifice - This sketch is the story logo. Let me tell you a story about a day that Yahweh annihilated a host of demon-worshiping prophets in Israel.

Sketch #2: False prophet - This sketch illustrates the first part of the story where Elijah and the people of Israel gather on Mount Carmel with the demon Baal's prophets.

Sketch #3: Fire - This sketch illustrates the second part of the story where Elijah prays, and Yahweh baptizes his water-soaked sacrifice altar with a flow of heavenly fire.

Sketch #4: Sword & cloud - This sketch illustrates the third part of the story where Elijah massacres the demon god's prophets, prays seven times for rain, and ends the drought.

### Storyteller Discipleship

The following activities will help you remember the story, apply wisdom to your own life, and tell the story to others.

- Listen to the story. Draw the story.
- Tell the story with the drawings.
- Draw your own pictures to illustrate the story.
- Pray and ask the Holy Spirit to reveal wisdom in the story.
- What is the Holy Spirit asking you to do next?
- Draw a map of your family and friends and pray for them.
- Go and tell the story to someone. Discuss the story.
- Disciple others to become Spirit-filled storytellers.

## Elijah's Heaven Ascension Story
2 Kings 2:1-22

Sketch #1: Elijah, Elisha, & mantle - This picture is the story logo. Let me tell you a story about a prophet that ascended to heaven in a fire chariot drawn by fire horses and angels.

Sketch #2: Elijah & Elisha - This sketch illustrates the first part of the story where Elijah prepares to go to heaven and asks Elisha to stay behind. Elisha remains with him.

Sketch #3: Elijah & fire chariot - This sketch illustrates the second part of the story where Elijah and Elisha cross the Jordan river. Elisha witnesses Elijah ascend to heaven.

Sketch #4: Elisha, mantle, & river - This sketch illustrates the third part of the story where Elisha receives a double portion of the Holy Spirit. He embraces Elijah's faith.

### Storyteller Discipleship

The following activities will help you remember the story, apply wisdom to your own life, and tell the story to others.

- Listen to the story. Draw the story.
- Tell the story with the drawings.
- Draw your own pictures to illustrate the story.
- Pray and ask the Holy Spirit to reveal wisdom in the story.
- What is the Holy Spirit asking you to do next?
- Draw a map of your family and friends and pray for them.
- Go and tell the story to someone. Discuss the story.
- Disciple others to become Spirit-filled storytellers.

## Elisha's Angel Army Story
### 2 Kings 6:8-23

Sketch #1: Cloud, chariot, & flame - This picture is the story logo. Let me tell you a story about a prophet's servant who saw an army of God's angels.

Sketch #2: Sword & shield - This sketch illustrates the first part of the story where the King of Aram sends his army to hunt down and destroy the prophet Elisha.

Sketch #3: Praying prophet - This sketch illustrates the second part of the story where Elisha prays for his servant to see, and God blinds the eyes of the Aramean soldiers.

Sketch #4: Table & food - This sketch illustrates the third part of the story where Elisha leads the Aramean army to the king of Israel. Israel feeds the army and makes peace.

### Storyteller Discipleship

The following activities will help you remember the story, apply wisdom to your own life, and tell the story to others.

- Listen to the story. Draw the story.
- Tell the story with the drawings.
- Draw your own pictures to illustrate the story.
- Pray and ask the Holy Spirit to reveal wisdom in the story.
- What is the Holy Spirit asking you to do next?
- Draw a map of your family and friends and pray for them.
- Go and tell the story to someone. Discuss the story.
- Disciple others to become Spirit-filled storytellers.

## Faithful Shepherd Song
### Psalms 23

Sketch #1: Crown, rod, & staff - This sketch is the song logo. Let me tell you about a song King David wrote describing God as our Faithful Shepherd and Loyal Guardian.

Sketch #2: Refreshed disciple - This sketch illustrates the first part of the song where Yahweh heals and cares for our lives as we enter into and enjoy his peaceful rest.

Sketch #3: Valley & flames - This sketch illustrates the second part of the song where Immanuel is with us as we journey through suffering in the power of the Holy Spirit.

Sketch #4: Overflowing fountain - This sketch illustrates the third part of the song where God anoints us with his favor and love, and we live together with him forever in Heaven.

## Storyteller Discipleship

The following activities will help you remember the story, apply wisdom to your own life, and tell the story to others.

- Listen to the story. Draw the story.
- Tell the story with the drawings.
- Draw your own pictures to illustrate the story.
- Pray and ask the Holy Spirit to reveal wisdom in the story.
- What is the Holy Spirit asking you to do next?
- Draw a map of your family and friends and pray for them.
- Go and tell the story to someone. Discuss the story.
- Disciple others to become Spirit-filled storytellers.

## Cursed Dragon's Fall Story
Ezekiel 28:1-19

Sketch #1: Snake & pit - This sketch is the story logo. Let me tell you a heartbreaking story about how God's greatest and most beautiful creation rebelled against him.

Sketch #2: Warrior angel - This sketch illustrates the first part of the story where Yahweh created the most beautiful angel named "Morning Star" and gave him great power.

Sketch #3: Throne & crown - This sketch illustrates the second part of the story where the Dragon became very wealthy, lusted after Yahweh's glory, and rebelled.

Sketch #4: Fire under water - This sketch illustrates the third part of the story where God threw the Dragon out of heaven and into the Lake of Fire in the heart of the sea.

### Storyteller Discipleship

The following activities will help you remember the story, apply wisdom to your own life, and tell the story to others.

- Listen to the story. Draw the story.
- Tell the story with the drawings.
- Draw your own pictures to illustrate the story.
- Pray and ask the Holy Spirit to reveal wisdom in the story.
- What is the Holy Spirit asking you to do next?
- Draw a map of your family and friends and pray for them.
- Go and tell the story to someone. Discuss the story.
- Disciple others to become Spirit-filled storytellers.

## Dry Bones Valley Story
Ezekiel 37:1-14

Sketch #1: Valley & bones - This picture is the story logo. Let me tell you a story about a valley full of bones.

Sketch #2: Bone - This sketch illustrates the first part of the vision where the Lord brings his prophet to a valley filled with bones and asks, "Son of man, can these bones live?"

Sketch #3: Prophet prophesying - This sketch illustrates the second part of the story where Ezekiel obeys the Lord's command to prophesy resurrection breath over the bones. They begin to shake, and the Lord covers them with flesh.

Sketch #4: Spirit-filled warrior - This sketch illustrates the third part of the story where the Lord redeems his people, gives them hope, and returns them to their land as warriors.

### Storyteller Discipleship

The following activities will help you remember the story, apply wisdom to your own life, and tell the story to others.

- Listen to the story. Draw the story.
- Tell the story with the drawings.
- Draw your own pictures to illustrate the story.
- Pray and ask the Holy Spirit to reveal wisdom in the story.
- What is the Holy Spirit asking you to do next?
- Draw a map of your family and friends and pray for them.
- Go and tell the story to someone. Discuss the story.
- Disciple others to become Spirit-filled storytellers.

## Life Healing River Story
Ezekiel 47:1-12

Sketch #1: Tree & river - This sketch is the story logo. Let me tell you a story about a living river that flows out of heaven to fill the earth with the presence and glory of God.

Sketch #2 - Water & depths - This sketch illustrates the first part of the story where Jesus coaches Ezekiel to swim in his Holy Spirit river and receive his anointing and power.

Sketch #3 - Fishing pole & fish - This sketch illustrates the second part of the story where Jesus tells Ezekiel that God's glory will be enjoyed by every nation and tribe.

Sketch #4: Healing fruit - This sketch illustrates the third part of the story where Jesus tells Ezekiel that Yahweh is faithful, and his kingdom fruit is provision and healing.

### Storyteller Discipleship

The following activities will help you remember the story, apply wisdom to your own life, and tell the story to others.

- Listen to the story. Draw the story.
- Tell the story with the drawings.
- Draw your own pictures to illustrate the story.
- Pray and ask the Holy Spirit to reveal wisdom in the story.
- What is the Holy Spirit asking you to do next?
- Draw a map of your family and friends and pray for them.
- Go and tell the story to someone. Discuss the story.
- Disciple others to become Spirit-filled storytellers.

## Babylon King's Gold Statue Story
### Daniel 3:1-30

<u>Sketch #1</u>: Idol & worshippers - This picture is the story logo. Let me tell you a story about a king who tried to make the whole world worship a gigantic statue of himself.

<u>Sketch #2</u>: Idol, pagan, & Jew - This sketch illustrates the first part of the story where the Babylonian leaders worship the statue, but Shadrach and his friends will not worship it.

<u>Sketch #3</u>: Flames - This sketch illustrates the second part of the story where King Nebuchadnezzar threatens the young men with death and throws them into the furnace.

<u>Sketch #4</u>: Open door - This sketch illustrates the third part of the story where the king sees an angel walking in the fire with the men. He releases them and begins to believe.

### Storyteller Discipleship

The following activities will help you remember the story, apply wisdom to your own life, and tell the story to others.

- Listen to the story. Draw the story.
- Tell the story with the drawings.
- Draw your own pictures to illustrate the story.
- Pray and ask the Holy Spirit to reveal wisdom in the story.
- What is the Holy Spirit asking you to do next?
- Draw a map of your family and friends and pray for them.
- Go and tell the story to someone. Discuss the story.
- Disciple others to become Spirit-filled storytellers.

**Pagan Beast King Story**
Daniel 4:1-37

Sketch #1: Tree & star - This sketch is the story logo. Let me tell you about a king who dreamed about a tree and became like a beast until he worshiped God.

Sketch #2: Cloud & tree - This sketch illustrates the first part of the story where King Nebuchadnezzar had a dream about the future, and Daniel interprets the dream.

Sketch #3: Beast - This sketch illustrates the second part of the story where the dream comes true. God humbles the king by making him like an animal for seven seasons.

Sketch #4: Praising king - This sketch illustrates the third part of the story where the king worships Yahweh as the only God. God returns his sanity and dominion back to him.

## Storyteller Discipleship

The following activities will help you remember the story, apply wisdom to your own life, and tell the story to others.

- Listen to the story. Draw the story.
- Tell the story with the drawings.
- Draw your own pictures to illustrate the story.
- Pray and ask the Holy Spirit to reveal wisdom in the story.
- What is the Holy Spirit asking you to do next?
- Draw a map of your family and friends and pray for them.
- Go and tell the story to someone. Discuss the story.
- Disciple others to become Spirit-filled storytellers.

## Lion's Den Deliverance Story
### Daniel 6:1-28

Sketch #1: Lion - This sketch is the story logo. Let me tell you a story about a faithful prophet who safely spent the night in a den of hungry lions.

Sketch #2: King - This sketch illustrates the first part of the story where King Darius orders everyone in his kingdom to worship him for a time.

Sketch #3: Lion's den - This sketch illustrates the second part of the story where Daniel is punished for disobeying the king and is miraculously untouched by the deadly lions.

Sketch #4: Cloud, throne, & crown - This sketch illustrates the third part of the story where King Darius repents and decrees Yahweh as God and worthy of worship.

## Storyteller Discipleship

The following activities will help you remember the story, apply wisdom to your own life, and tell the story to others.

- Listen to the story. Draw the story.
- Tell the story with the drawings.
- Draw your own pictures to illustrate the story.
- Pray and ask the Holy Spirit to reveal wisdom in the story.
- What is the Holy Spirit asking you to do next?
- Draw a map of your family and friends and pray for them.
- Go and tell the story to someone. Discuss the story.
- Disciple others to become Spirit-filled storytellers.

**Jonah's Whale Adventure Story**
Jonah 1:1 - 2:10

Sketch #1: Fish & prophet - This picture is the story logo. Let me tell you a story about a rebellious prophet who wrote a worship song inside a whale belly.

Sketch #2: Boat & Jonah - This sketch illustrates the first part of the story where Jonah disobeys God's commands and runs away on a ship.

Sketch #3: Storm & waves - This sketch illustrates the second part of the story where the sailors throw Jonah into the sea, and God sends a great fish to rescue his prophet.

Sketch #4: Jonah & water song - This sketch illustrates the third part of the story where Jonah writes a worship song about God's salvation and deliverance.

### Storyteller Discipleship

The following activities will help you remember the story, apply wisdom to your own life, and tell the story to others.

- Listen to the story. Draw the story.
- Tell the story with the drawings.
- Draw your own pictures to illustrate the story.
- Pray and ask the Holy Spirit to reveal wisdom in the story.
- What is the Holy Spirit asking you to do next?
- Draw a map of your family and friends and pray for them.
- Go and tell the story to someone. Discuss the story.
- Disciple others to become Spirit-filled storytellers.

**John Baptizes Jesus Story**
Matthew 3:13-17

Sketch #1: Water & Jesus - This sketch is the story logo. Let me tell you a story about how John the Baptizer experienced the joy of baptizing God's Messiah.

Sketch #2: John & Jesus - This sketch illustrates the first part of the story where Jesus visits John and requests baptism. John was hesitant, because he knew Jesus is holy.

Sketch #3: Baptism waters - This sketch illustrates the second part of the story where John baptizes Jesus.

Sketch #4: Yahweh speaks - This sketch illustrates the third part of the story where God the Father sends the Holy Spirit as a sign, speaks from heaven, and blesses his Son.

**Storyteller Discipleship**

The following activities will help you remember the story, apply wisdom to your own life, and tell the story to others.

- Listen to the story. Draw the story.
- Tell the story with the drawings.
- Draw your own pictures to illustrate the story.
- Pray and ask the Holy Spirit to reveal wisdom in the story.
- What is the Holy Spirit asking you to do next?
- Draw a map of your family and friends and pray for them.
- Go and tell the story to someone. Discuss the story.
- Disciple others to become Spirit-filled storytellers.

## Satan Tempts Jesus Story
Matthew 4:1-11

Sketch #1: Snake & crown - This sketch is the story logo. Let me tell you a story about how the evil dragon visited Jesus in the wilderness and tried to manipulate him into rebellion.

Sketch #2: Bread - This sketch illustrates the first temptation where Satan asks Jesus to turn stones into bread.

Sketch #3: Angel - This sketch illustrates the second temptation where Satan asks Jesus to throw himself off the Jerusalem temple and prove he is God's Son.

Sketch #4: Mountain - This sketch illustrates the third temptation where Satan offers to make Jesus the king of the whole world if he will deny God and worship him.

## Storyteller Discipleship

The following activities will help you remember the story, apply wisdom to your own life, and tell the story to others.

- Listen to the story. Draw the story.
- Tell the story with the drawings.
- Draw your own pictures to illustrate the story.
- Pray and ask the Holy Spirit to reveal wisdom in the story.
- What is the Holy Spirit asking you to do next?
- Draw a map of your family and friends and pray for them.
- Go and tell the story to someone. Discuss the story.
- Disciple others to become Spirit-filled storytellers.

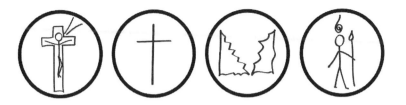

**Jesus Christ Dies Story**
Matthew 27:45-56

Sketch #1: Jesus crying out - This sketch is the story logo. Let me tell you a story about the day Jesus Messiah died.

Sketch #2: Cross - This sketch illustrates the first part of the story where Jesus dies on the cross.

Sketch #3: Torn veil - This sketch illustrates the second part of the story where many signs accompanied Jesus' death such as an earthquake, the dead raised, and the torn temple veil.

Sketch #4: Roman soldier - This sketch illustrates the third part of the story where Jesus' family and friends wept at his death, and the pagan Roman soldier believed in Jesus as God's Son.

### Storyteller Discipleship

The following activities will help you remember the story, apply wisdom to your own life, and tell the story to others.

- Listen to the story. Draw the story.
- Tell the story with the drawings.
- Draw your own pictures to illustrate the story.
- Pray and ask the Holy Spirit to reveal wisdom in the story.
- What is the Holy Spirit asking you to do next?
- Draw a map of your family and friends and pray for them.
- Go and tell the story to someone. Discuss the story.
- Disciple others to become Spirit-filled storytellers.

## Four Soils Story
Mark 4:1-20

Sketch #1: Farmer sowing seeds - This picture is the story logo. Let me tell you a story about a farmer who sowed seeds on four different soils.

Sketch #2: Seed & soil: This sketch illustrates the first part of the story where Jesus teaches and begins this story with a farmer who sows seed on hard soil.

Sketch #3: Rocks & thorns: This sketch illustrates the second part of the story where Jesus describes the second and third types of receptive but unfruitful soils.

Sketch #4: Plant & roots - This sketch illustrates the third part of the story where Jesus describes the healthy fourth soil that bears a fruitful, multiplying crop.

## Storyteller Discipleship

The following activities will help you remember the story, apply wisdom to your own life, and tell the story to others.

- Listen to the story. Draw the story.
- Tell the story with the drawings.
- Draw your own pictures to illustrate the story.
- Pray and ask the Holy Spirit to reveal wisdom in the story.
- What is the Holy Spirit asking you to do next?
- Draw a map of your family and friends and pray for them.
- Go and tell the story to someone. Discuss the story.
- Disciple others to become Spirit-filled storytellers.

## Calming The Storm Story
### Mark 4:35-41

Sketch #1: Jesus, boat, sea, & storm — This sketch is the story logo. Let me tell you a story about a storm that listened to Jesus.

Sketch #2: Jesus, disciples, & boat — This sketch illustrates the first part of the story where Jesus and his disciples leave the crowds and begin to sail across the sea.

Sketch #3: Cloud & lightning bolt — This sketch illustrates the second part of the story where the disciples wake up Jesus. He calms the storm and sea.

Sketch #4: Sun & water — This sketch illustrates the third part of the story where the calm sea and clear day resulted from Jesus' authority and power over nature.

### Storyteller Discipleship

The following activities will help you remember the story, apply wisdom to your own life, and tell the story to others.

- Listen to the story. Draw the story.
- Tell the story with the drawings.
- Draw your own pictures to illustrate the story.
- Pray and ask the Holy Spirit to reveal wisdom in the story.
- What is the Holy Spirit asking you to do next?
- Draw a map of your family and friends and pray for them.
- Go and tell the story to someone. Discuss the story.
- Disciple others to become Spirit-filled storytellers.

## Demon Army Exorcism Story
### Mark 5:1-20

Sketch #1: Jesus, man, & tomb - This sketch is the story logo. Let me tell you a story about Jesus exorcizing 4,000 evil spirits out of one man's body so he would be free.

Sketch #2: Man - This sketch illustrates the first part of the story where Jesus and his disciples encounter the possessed man, and Jesus talks to the demons.

Sketch #3: Pig & snake - This sketch illustrates the second part of the story where Jesus delivers the man, a great herd of pigs drown in the lake, and the locals ask Jesus to leave.

Sketch #4: Man & cities - This sketch illustrates the third part of the story where the delivered man tries to follow Jesus. He sends the man to ten cities to share his story.

### Storyteller Discipleship

The following activities will help you remember the story, apply wisdom to your own life, and tell the story to others.

- Listen to the story. Draw the story.
- Tell the story with the drawings.
- Draw your own pictures to illustrate the story.
- Pray and ask the Holy Spirit to reveal wisdom in the story.
- What is the Holy Spirit asking you to do next?
- Draw a map of your family and friends and pray for them.
- Go and tell the story to someone. Discuss the story.
- Disciple others to become Spirit-filled storytellers.

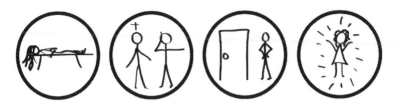

## Dead Girl Resurrection Story
### Mark 5:21-43

Sketch #1: Dead girl - This sketch is the story logo. Let me tell you a story about how Jesus raised a dead girl to life.

Sketch #2: Jesus & Jairus - This sketch illustrates the first part of the story where Jairus came to Jesus and asked him to visit his home and heal his daughter on her deathbed.

Sketch #3: Closed door & mourner - This sketch illustrates the second part of the story where Jesus makes those mourning the girl's death stay outside during his visit.

Sketch #4: Restored girl - This sketch illustrates the third part of the story where Jesus miraculously resurrects Jairus' daughter and demonstrates his divine power over death.

### Storyteller Discipleship

The following activities will help you remember the story, apply wisdom to your own life, and tell the story to others.

- Listen to the story. Draw the story.
- Tell the story with the drawings.
- Draw your own pictures to illustrate the story.
- Pray and ask the Holy Spirit to reveal wisdom in the story.
- What is the Holy Spirit asking you to do next?
- Draw a map of your family and friends and pray for them.
- Go and tell the story to someone. Discuss the story.
- Disciple others to become Spirit-filled storytellers.

## Bleeding Woman Healed Story
### Mark 5:24-34

Sketch #1: Woman & cloak - This sketch is the story logo. Let me tell you a story about how Jesus healed a despairing woman sick with 12 years of chronic bleeding.

Sketch #2: Sick woman - This sketch illustrates the first part of the story where the woman is in the crowds and reaches out to touch Jesus' cloak.

Sketch #3: Freedom & broken chains - This sketch illustrates the second part of the story where the sick woman is miraculously healed.

Sketch #4: Jesus confused - This sketch illustrates the third part of the story where Jesus searches for and finds the woman and blesses her leap of faith.

### Storyteller Discipleship

The following activities will help you remember the story, apply wisdom to your own life, and tell the story to others.

- Listen to the story. Draw the story.
- Tell the story with the drawings.
- Draw your own pictures to illustrate the story.
- Pray and ask the Holy Spirit to reveal wisdom in the story.
- What is the Holy Spirit asking you to do next?
- Draw a map of your family and friends and pray for them.
- Go and tell the story to someone. Discuss the story.
- Disciple others to become Spirit-filled storytellers.

**Foot Washing Prostitute Story**
Luke 7:36-50

<u>Sketch #1</u>: Jesus & woman - This picture is the story logo. Let me tell you a story about a prostitute who honored Jesus by washing his feet with her tears.

<u>Sketch #2</u>: Tears & perfume bottle - This sketch illustrates the first part of the story where Jesus eats with Simon and the prostitute comes in to wash the Lord's feet.

<u>Sketch #3</u>: Money bag & coins - This sketch illustrates the second part of the story where Simon is upset, and Jesus tells his friend a story about forgiveness.

<u>Sketch #4</u>: Broken chain & woman - This sketch illustrates the third part of the story where Jesus forgives the woman and sets this captive free!

## Storyteller Discipleship

The following activities will help you remember the story, apply wisdom to your own life, and tell the story to others.

- Listen to the story. Draw the story.
- Tell the story with the drawings.
- Draw your own pictures to illustrate the story.
- Pray and ask the Holy Spirit to reveal wisdom in the story.
- What is the Holy Spirit asking you to do next?
- Draw a map of your family and friends and pray for them.
- Go and tell the story to someone. Discuss the story.
- Disciple others to become Spirit-filled storytellers.

## Peace House Mission Story
Luke 10:1-20

<u>Sketch #1</u>: house & open door - This sketch is the story logo. Let me tell you a story about Jesus sending teams of his disciples out to visit local villages and set people free.

<u>Sketch #2</u>: praying disciples - This sketch illustrates mission teams praying together. Before we go into the Lord's harvest, we ask him to set apart and send more workers.

<u>Sketch #3</u>: road over water - This sketch illustrates our faith journey to reach other nations and cultures. God is our Companion and Navigator, our Protector and Provider.

<u>Sketch #4</u>: disciple & flame - This sketch illustrates God's peace invitation. We enter homes open to us and our Prince of Peace. We invite them to receive the Holy Spirit.

### Storyteller Discipleship

The following activities will help you remember the story, apply wisdom to your own life, and tell the story to others.

- Listen to the story. Draw the story.
- Tell the story with the drawings.
- Draw your own pictures to illustrate the story.
- Pray and ask the Holy Spirit to reveal wisdom in the story.
- What is the Holy Spirit asking you to do next?
- Draw a map of your family and friends and pray for them.
- Go and tell the story to someone. Discuss the story.
- Disciple others to become Spirit-filled storytellers.

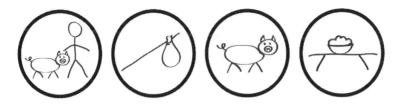

## Lost Son Story
### Luke 15:11-32

<u>Sketch #1</u>: Son & pig - This sketch is the story logo. Let me tell you a story about a wealthy family who lost their son.

<u>Sketch #2</u>: Stick & travel bag - This sketch illustrates the first part of the story where the lost son asks for his inheritance early and travels to a foreign land alone.

<u>Sketch #3</u>: Pig - This sketch illustrates the second part of the story where the lost son becomes the starving servant of a pig farmer.

<u>Sketch #4</u>: Table & meal - This sketch illustrates the third part of the story where the father forgives his lost son and explains his decision to the angry, jealous brother.

## Storyteller Discipleship

The following activities will help you remember the story, apply wisdom to your own life, and tell the story to others.

- Listen to the story. Draw the story.
- Tell the story with the drawings.
- Draw your own pictures to illustrate the story.
- Pray and ask the Holy Spirit to reveal wisdom in the story.
- What is the Holy Spirit asking you to do next?
- Draw a map of your family and friends and pray for them.
- Go and tell the story to someone. Discuss the story.
- Disciple others to become Spirit-filled storytellers.

## Generous Tax Collector Story
Luke 19:1-10

Sketch #1: Zacchaeus & Jesus - This sketch is the story logo. Let me tell you a story about a greedy tax collector who became generous after eating dinner with Jesus.

Sketch #2: Tree - This sketch illustrates the first part of the story where Jesus is traveling through Jericho and encounters Zacchaeus sitting up high in a tree.

Sketch #3: Dinner table - This sketch illustrates the second part of the story where Jesus eats with Zacchaeus in his home and teaches him about Yahweh's kingdom.

Sketch #4: Money bag - This sketch illustrates the third part of the story where Zacchaeus repents of his sins and makes a generosity plan. Jesus forgives him.

## Storyteller Discipleship

The following activities will help you remember the story, apply wisdom to your own life, and tell the story to others.

- Listen to the story. Draw the story.
- Tell the story with the drawings.
- Draw your own pictures to illustrate the story.
- Pray and ask the Holy Spirit to reveal wisdom in the story.
- What is the Holy Spirit asking you to do next?
- Draw a map of your family and friends and pray for them.
- Go and tell the story to someone. Discuss the story.
- Disciple others to become Spirit-filled storytellers.

## Widow's Faith Gift Story
### Luke 20:45 - 21:4

Sketch #1: Woman & two coins - This sketch is the story logo. Let me tell you a story about a widow with legendary faith.

Sketch #2: Two men - This sketch illustrates the first part of the story where religious leaders and the rich aspire to be praised and rewarded by men.

Sketch #3: Money bag & two coins - This sketch illustrates the second part of the story where the rich gave large gifts publicly, and the widow humbly gave two small coins.

Sketch #4: Cloud & bread - This sketch illustrates the third part of the story where Jesus revealed that the widow trusted her Father in heaven to provide her daily bread.

## Storyteller Discipleship

The following activities will help you remember the story, apply wisdom to your own life, and tell the story to others.

- Listen to the story. Draw the story.
- Tell the story with the drawings.
- Draw your own pictures to illustrate the story.
- Pray and ask the Holy Spirit to reveal wisdom in the story.
- What is the Holy Spirit asking you to do next?
- Draw a map of your family and friends and pray for them.
- Go and tell the story to someone. Discuss the story.
- Disciple others to become Spirit-filled storytellers.

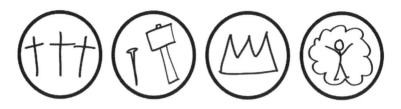

### Jesus Christ Crucified Story
Luke 23:26-43

Sketch #1: Three crosses - This sketch is the story logo. Let me tell you a story about the Savior of the world being nailed to a cross between two convicted thieves.

Sketch #2: Hammer & nail - This sketch illustrates the first part of the story where Roman soldiers nailed Jesus of Nazareth to a cross.

Sketch #3: Crown - This sketch illustrates the second part of the story where several people witnessing Jesus' death mocked him for claiming to be Messiah and King.

Sketch #4: Cloud & man - This sketch illustrates the third part of the story where Jesus prophesies that the repentant criminal will be with him in heaven that same day.

### Storyteller Discipleship

The following activities will help you remember the story, apply wisdom to your own life, and tell the story to others.

- Listen to the story. Draw the story.
- Tell the story with the drawings.
- Draw your own pictures to illustrate the story.
- Pray and ask the Holy Spirit to reveal wisdom in the story.
- What is the Holy Spirit asking you to do next?
- Draw a map of your family and friends and pray for them.
- Go and tell the story to someone. Discuss the story.
- Disciple others to become Spirit-filled storytellers.

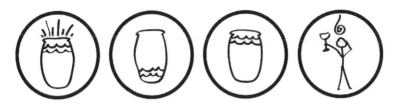

## Water Becomes Wine Story
### John 2:1-11

Sketch #1: Miracle wine - This sketch is the story logo. Let me tell you a story about Jesus turning 100 gallons of water into delicious wine as a wedding gift.

Sketch #2: Empty jar - This sketch illustrates the first part of the story where the wedding feast ran out of wine, and Mary requests a miracle from her son.

Sketch #3: Full jar - This sketch illustrates the second part of the story where Jesus changes the full jars of water into over 100 gallons of delicious wine.

Sketch #4: Chief servant - This sketch illustrates the third part of the story where the chief servant praises the groom for saving the best wine for the end of the celebration.

## Storyteller Discipleship

The following activities will help you remember the story, apply wisdom to your own life, and tell the story to others.

- Listen to the story. Draw the story.
- Tell the story with the drawings.
- Draw your own pictures to illustrate the story.
- Pray and ask the Holy Spirit to reveal wisdom in the story.
- What is the Holy Spirit asking you to do next?
- Draw a map of your family and friends and pray for them.
- Go and tell the story to someone. Discuss the story.
- Disciple others to become Spirit-filled storytellers.

**Samaritan Village Revival Story**
John 4:1-42

Sketch #1: Water well - This sketch is the story logo. Let me tell you a story about how Jesus led a whole village to faith in God beside a well.

Sketch #2: Woman - This sketch illustrates the first part of the story where Jesus starts a spiritual conversation with the rejected woman.

Sketch #3: Animal sacrifice - This sketch illustrates the second part of the story where Jesus and the woman discuss different forms of worship.

Sketch #4: Wheat bundle - This sketch illustrates the third part of the story where the woman leads her entire village to faith in Jesus, and a spiritual revival takes place!

### Storyteller Discipleship

The following activities will help you remember the story, apply wisdom to your own life, and tell the story to others.

- Listen to the story. Draw the story.
- Tell the story with the drawings.
- Draw your own pictures to illustrate the story.
- Pray and ask the Holy Spirit to reveal wisdom in the story.
- What is the Holy Spirit asking you to do next?
- Draw a map of your family and friends and pray for them.
- Go and tell the story to someone. Discuss the story.
- Disciple others to become Spirit-filled storytellers.

## Official's Son Healing Story
John 4:46-54

Sketch #1: Healed son - This sketch is the story logo. Let me tell you a story about Jesus healing a royal man's sick son.

Sketch #2: Sick son - This sketch illustrates the first part of the story where the royal official travels to find Jesus and begs him to come to his house and heal his son.

Sketch #3: Jesus & broken chains - This sketch illustrates the second part of the story where Jesus tells the man to go home, because he has already healed his son.

Sketch #4: Believing house - This sketch illustrates the third part of the story where the royal official and his entire family witness God's power and believe in Jesus as Messiah.

## Storyteller Discipleship

The following activities will help you remember the story, apply wisdom to your own life, and tell the story to others.

- Listen to the story. Draw the story.
- Tell the story with the drawings.
- Draw your own pictures to illustrate the story.
- Pray and ask the Holy Spirit to reveal wisdom in the story.
- What is the Holy Spirit asking you to do next?
- Draw a map of your family and friends and pray for them.
- Go and tell the story to someone. Discuss the story.
- Disciple others to become Spirit-filled storytellers.

### Bethesda Pool Healing Story
John 5:1-18

Sketch #1: Angel over water - This sketch is the story logo. Let me tell you a story about a pool where people believed that visiting angels touched the water to heal the sick.

Sketch #2: Glowing water - This sketch illustrates the first part of the story where Jesus visits the Bethesda Pool on a Sabbath day to heal the sick.

Sketch #3: Healed man - This sketch illustrates the second part of the story where Jesus miraculously heals the man, and he reports this sign to the Jewish authorities.

Sketch #4: Jesus & Yahweh - This sketch illustrates the third part of the story where the Jews begin strategizing how to kill Jesus, because he called Yahweh his "Father."

### Storyteller Discipleship

The following activities will help you remember the story, apply wisdom to your own life, and tell the story to others.

- Listen to the story. Draw the story.
- Tell the story with the drawings.
- Draw your own pictures to illustrate the story.
- Pray and ask the Holy Spirit to reveal wisdom in the story.
- What is the Holy Spirit asking you to do next?
- Draw a map of your family and friends and pray for them.
- Go and tell the story to someone. Discuss the story.
- Disciple others to become Spirit-filled storytellers.

## Fish And Bread Feast Story
John 6:1-15

Sketch #1: Fish & loaf - This sketch is the story logo. Let me tell you a story about how Jesus fed 5,000 men and their families with two fish and five loaves of bread.

Sketch #2: Jesus & boy - This sketch illustrates the first part of the story where Jesus instructs the disciples to feed the crowd, and a little boy offers his lunch to them.

Sketch #3: Feast - This sketch illustrates the second part of the story where Jesus prayed over the meal, and his disciples fed all 5,000 men and their families.

Sketch #4: Cloud & crown - This sketch illustrates the third part of the story where the crowd tries to make Jesus their king, and he escapes to the mountain to be alone.

## Storyteller Discipleship

The following activities will help you remember the story, apply wisdom to your own life, and tell the story to others.

- Listen to the story. Draw the story.
- Tell the story with the drawings.
- Draw your own pictures to illustrate the story.
- Pray and ask the Holy Spirit to reveal wisdom in the story.
- What is the Holy Spirit asking you to do next?
- Draw a map of your family and friends and pray for them.
- Go and tell the story to someone. Discuss the story.
- Disciple others to become Spirit-filled storytellers.

## Walking On Water Story
### John 6:16-21

Sketch #1: Jesus on water - This sketch is the story logo. Let me tell you a story about how Jesus rescued his disciples from drowning by walking on water.

Sketch #2: Boat - This sketch illustrates the first part of the story where Jesus' disciples waited for their Master and then decided to sail home at night when He did not return.

Sketch #3: Wind - This sketch illustrates the second part of the story where the disciples became lost in a raging storm. They saw Jesus walking on water and were afraid.

Sketch #4: Believing disciple - This sketch illustrates the third part of the story where Jesus' disciples witness Him transport their boat instantly across a great distance.

### Storyteller Discipleship

The following activities will help you remember the story, apply wisdom to your own life, and tell the story to others.

- Listen to the story. Draw the story.
- Tell the story with the drawings.
- Draw your own pictures to illustrate the story.
- Pray and ask the Holy Spirit to reveal wisdom in the story.
- What is the Holy Spirit asking you to do next?
- Draw a map of your family and friends and pray for them.
- Go and tell the story to someone. Discuss the story.
- Disciple others to become Spirit-filled storytellers.

## Blind Beggar Healing Story
### John 9:1-41

Sketch #1: Blind man - This sketch is the story logo. Let me tell you a story about Jesus healing a poor, blind beggar.

Sketch #2: Water - This sketch illustrates the first part of the story where Jesus rubs spit and mud on the beggar's eyes. He washes in a pool called "Sent," and he sees. Hallelujah!

Sketch #3: Witness - This sketch illustrates the second part of the story where the man is healed and boldly declares his miracle testimony to the local governing leaders.

Sketch #4: Judge gavel - This sketch illustrates the third part of the story where the local leaders judged the man evil, but Jesus judged him as faithful and blessed him.

### Storyteller Discipleship

The following activities will help you remember the story, apply wisdom to your own life, and tell the story to others.

- Listen to the story. Draw the story.
- Tell the story with the drawings.
- Draw your own pictures to illustrate the story.
- Pray and ask the Holy Spirit to reveal wisdom in the story.
- What is the Holy Spirit asking you to do next?
- Draw a map of your family and friends and pray for them.
- Go and tell the story to someone. Discuss the story.
- Disciple others to become Spirit-filled storytellers.

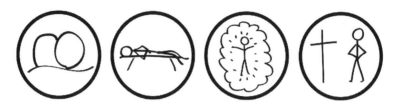

**Jesus Resurrects Lazarus Story**
John 11:1-57

Sketch #1: Empty tomb - This sketch is the story logo. Let me tell you about Jesus resurrecting one of his best friends.

Sketch #2: Dead man - This sketch illustrates the first part of the story where Lazarus becomes sick and dies. Jesus waits for him to die, and then he goes to visit his family.

Sketch #3: Resurrection - This sketch illustrates the second part of the story where Jesus talks to Mary and Martha and resurrects Lazarus.

Sketch #4: Cross & priest - This sketch illustrates the third part of the story where many believed in Jesus. The religious leaders rejected Jesus and planned his crucifixion.

## Storyteller Discipleship

The following activities will help you remember the story, apply wisdom to your own life, and tell the story to others.

- Listen to the story. Draw the story.
- Tell the story with the drawings.
- Draw your own pictures to illustrate the story.
- Pray and ask the Holy Spirit to reveal wisdom in the story.
- What is the Holy Spirit asking you to do next?
- Draw a map of your family and friends and pray for them.
- Go and tell the story to someone. Discuss the story.
- Disciple others to become Spirit-filled storytellers.

## Remain In Me Story
John 15:1-17

Sketch #1: Vineyard keeper & vine - This sketch is the story logo. Let me tell you a story about how God wants us to rest in his presence every day so we can be free.

Sketch #2: Vine, branches, & fruit - This sketch illustrates Jesus as our Master and Source of Life. The fruitful branch is a disciple who remains in Jesus and obeys him.

Sketch #3: Burning branches - This sketch illustrates the Father cutting off branches unreceptive to living water. They burn up and are blown away, because they are dead.

Sketch #4: Crucified Christ - This sketch illustrates the love of Jesus for us: he gave his life as a sign of perfect love, and he invites his disciples to lay down their lives as well.

## Storyteller Discipleship

The following activities will help you remember the story, apply wisdom to your own life, and tell the story to others.

- Listen to the story. Draw the story.
- Tell the story with the drawings.
- Draw your own pictures to illustrate the story.
- Pray and ask the Holy Spirit to reveal wisdom in the story.
- What is the Holy Spirit asking you to do next?
- Draw a map of your family and friends and pray for them.
- Go and tell the story to someone. Discuss the story.
- Disciple others to become Spirit-filled storytellers.

## Jesus Is Alive Story
John 20:1-18

Sketch #1: Empty tomb - This sketch is the story logo. Let me tell you a story about Jesus' resurrection after his death.

Sketch #2: Running man - This sketch illustrates the first part of the story where Mary ran to tell Peter and John about the empty tomb, and they ran to investigate.

Sketch #3: Crying woman - This sketch illustrates the second part of the story where Mary stays in the garden confused and crying. Two angels reveal themselves and speak with her.

Sketch #4: Risen Christ - This sketch illustrates the third part of the story where Jesus reveals himself to Mary. She is overjoyed and returns to tell the other disciples the news.

### Storyteller Discipleship

The following activities will help you remember the story, apply wisdom to your own life, and tell the story to others.

- Listen to the story. Draw the story.
- Tell the story with the drawings.
- Draw your own pictures to illustrate the story.
- Pray and ask the Holy Spirit to reveal wisdom in the story.
- What is the Holy Spirit asking you to do next?
- Draw a map of your family and friends and pray for them.
- Go and tell the story to someone. Discuss the story.
- Disciple others to become Spirit-filled storytellers.

## Pentecost Day Miracle Story
Acts 2:1-13

Sketch #1: Man, woman, & flames - This sketch is the story logo. Let me tell you a story about the day Jesus sent the Holy Spirit in power to live with his first disciples.

Sketch #2: House & wind - This sketch illustrates the first part of the story where Jesus visits the disciples. Our Lord breathes on them, and they receive the Holy Spirit.

Sketch #3: Disciple preaching - This sketch illustrates the second part of the story where the disciples preach the gospel in many languages to the nations in Jerusalem.

Sketch #4: Two reactions - This sketch illustrates the third part of the story where some people who listen believe the gospel, while others harden their hearts towards Jesus.

## Storyteller Discipleship

The following activities will help you remember the story, apply wisdom to your own life, and tell the story to others.

- Listen to the story. Draw the story.
- Tell the story with the drawings.
- Draw your own pictures to illustrate the story.
- Pray and ask the Holy Spirit to reveal wisdom in the story.
- What is the Holy Spirit asking you to do next?
- Draw a map of your family and friends and pray for them.
- Go and tell the story to someone. Discuss the story.
- Disciple others to become Spirit-filled storytellers.

## Philip Baptizes Official Story
Acts 8:26-40

Sketch #1: Philip & whirlwind - This sketch is the story logo. Let me tell you a story about how Jesus transported one of his disciples on mission trips in a whirlwind.

Sketch #2: Philip & road - This sketch illustrates the first part of the story where Philip obeys the angel of the Lord and goes to the desert road to disciple the official.

Sketch #3: Philip, official, & water - This sketch illustrates the second part of the story where the official requests baptism, and Philip baptizes the new believer.

Sketch #4: Philip preaching & villages - This sketch illustrates the third part of the story where the Holy Spirit miraculously transports Philip to Azotus on a new mission.

### Storyteller Discipleship

The following activities will help you remember the story, apply wisdom to your own life, and tell the story to others.

- Listen to the story. Draw the story.
- Tell the story with the drawings.
- Draw your own pictures to illustrate the story.
- Pray and ask the Holy Spirit to reveal wisdom in the story.
- What is the Holy Spirit asking you to do next?
- Draw a map of your family and friends and pray for them.
- Go and tell the story to someone. Discuss the story.
- Disciple others to become Spirit-filled storytellers.

**Jesus Saves Paul Story**
Acts 9:1-20

Sketch #1: Cloud & Jesus - This sketch is the story logo. Let me tell you a story about how a man who hated Christians met Jesus face to face and became a missionary.

Sketch #2: Paul, chains, and prisoner - This sketch illustrates the first part of the story where Paul journeys to Damascus to imprison Jesus followers in that city.

Sketch #3: Blind man - This sketch illustrates the second part of the story where Jesus instructs Ananias to visit Paul, heal him of blindness, and baptize him in the Holy Spirit.

Sketch #4: Baptism waters - This sketch illustrates the third part of the story where Paul decides to follow Jesus, be baptized, and begin his new life as a living sacrifice.

**Storyteller Discipleship**

The following activities will help you remember the story, apply wisdom to your own life, and tell the story to others.

• Listen to the story. Draw the story.
• Tell the story with the drawings.
• Draw your own pictures to illustrate the story.
• Pray and ask the Holy Spirit to reveal wisdom in the story.
• What is the Holy Spirit asking you to do next?
• Draw a map of your family and friends and pray for them.
• Go and tell the story to someone. Discuss the story.
• Disciple others to become Spirit-filled storytellers.

**Enter My Rest Story**
Hebrews 4:1-13

Sketch #1: Open door & river - This sketch is the story logo. Let me tell you a story about a special sanctuary God made for us to rest and refresh in his presence.

Sketch #2: Cloud & dawn - This sketch illustrates God modeling sabbath rest for his people. He created everything in six days; then, he rested on the seventh day.

Sketch #3: Crown, barrier, & heart - This sketch illustrates a person rejecting God's command to rest. We do not only listen to him, we also love, obey, and enjoy his Spirit.

Sketch #4: Sword & heart - This sketch illustrates Jesus Christ as God's Word. His truth and resurrection life penetrates our hearts, reveals sin, and sets us free!

## Storyteller Discipleship

The following activities will help you remember the story, apply wisdom to your own life, and tell the story to others.

- Listen to the story. Draw the story.
- Tell the story with the drawings.
- Draw your own pictures to illustrate the story.
- Pray and ask the Holy Spirit to reveal wisdom in the story.
- What is the Holy Spirit asking you to do next?
- Draw a map of your family and friends and pray for them.
- Go and tell the story to someone. Discuss the story.
- Disciple others to become Spirit-filled storytellers.

## Thunder Voice Angel Story
### Revelation 10:1-7

Sketch #1: Angel, cloud, & rainbow - This sketch is the story logo. Let me tell you a story about a colossal angel whose voice sounds like thunder and wears a rainbow halo.

Sketch #2: Angel, sea, & land - This sketch illustrates the first part of the story where John witnesses the angel approaching and describes him.

Sketch #3: Lightning bolt - This sketch illustrates the second part of the story where the angel shouts and seven thunders prophesy.

Sketch #4: Blowing trumpet - This sketch illustrates the third part of the story where the angel prophesies a seventh angel who blows a trumpet, and Yahweh's plan is fulfilled.

## Storyteller Discipleship

The following activities will help you remember the story, apply wisdom to your own life, and tell the story to others.

- Listen to the story. Draw the story.
- Tell the story with the drawings.
- Draw your own pictures to illustrate the story.
- Pray and ask the Holy Spirit to reveal wisdom in the story.
- What is the Holy Spirit asking you to do next?
- Draw a map of your family and friends and pray for them.
- Go and tell the story to someone. Discuss the story.
- Disciple others to become Spirit-filled storytellers.

STORYTELLERS
BIBLE
PROJECT

## Authors

Hello, my name is James Harvey. I am a missionary kid who grew up in China and the Philippines. I have traveled around the world and have a deep love for all peoples.

Draw Disciples is the first publication in a series of books we plan to develop and publish for the storyteller movement. I believe that all we need to reach the world with Jesus' message is our Father's love, Bible stories, and the Holy Spirit. I pray that our lessons and drawings will inspire you to pray for all nations and tell others his stories.

Hello, my name is Brian Hayden. I am an artist living in Jensen Beach, Florida. Until a few years ago, my work was most known in the fishing industry. My artwork has been featured at the International Game Fishing Hall of Fame Museum and in many fishing publications globally. I have often prayed for my artwork to be used for the glory of God. I met James through the No Place Left network, and we became friends. Since then, I have created hundreds of No Place Left regional logos for mission teams and dozens of field tools for leaders and agencies all over the world. My recent work has revolved around the Orality Bible Project which you can see at oralitybible.com. Now, my artwork is less about fishing for fish and more focused on fishing for men and women to become followers of Jesus Christ.

## Blazing Trees

Blazing Trees is a 501(c)(3) charity organization based in Nashville, TN that innovates mission resources and provides prayer, encouragement, and coaching to leaders and their teams scattered across the nations.

In 2015, we experienced the following vision that led us to launch our organization:

I was standing in a forest watching a man try to start a fire with rocks. The forest had recently been washed in a rainstorm, so the ground and wood were soaking wet.

The man was using two small flint rocks to try to spark a fire. I could hear the rocks cracking as he hit them together over and over again. The piercing snaps echoed cascading sound waves into the damp evening air. He was deliberate in every move of his hands, and where others would give up, this man was unwavering in attempting to start this fire.

All of a sudden, one of the sparks caught the wood on fire, and it began to blaze. The flames slowly grew stronger and higher until some of the embers from the fire floated up into the trees, and they began to catch the leaves and limbs on fire. Soon trees were fully ablaze, and the embers from the first blazing trees floated into the air and came to rest upon other nearby trees catching them on fire as well. None of the trees were burning up or being consumed by the heat.

I raised up into the night sky and saw the forest blazing brightly, further than my eyes could see in every direction: a movement of fire, warmth, and glorious light.

To learn more, please visit blazingtrees.org.

# Recommendations

Our development and design team highly recommends these helpful discipleship resources for you to investigate:

| | |
|---|---|
| Movements that Change the World | Steve Addison |
| What Jesus Started | Steve Addison |
| Bondage Breaker | Neil Anderson |
| Misfits Welcome | Matthew Barnett |
| Indigenous Church Planting | Charles Brock |
| The Rest of God | Mark Buchanan |
| Forgotten God | Francis Chan |
| Organic Church | Neil Cole |
| Search & Rescue | Neil Cole |
| The Calvary Road | Roy Hession |
| Needless Casualties of War | John Paul Jackson |
| Practicing the Presence of God | Brother Lawrence |
| 21 Irrefutable Laws of Leadership | John Maxwell |
| A Work of Heart | Reggie McNeal |
| Radical Together | David Platt |
| The Universe Next Door | James Sire |
| Instruments in the Redeemer's Hands | Paul David Tripp |
| Whiter than Snow | Paul David Tripp |
| The Bible Jesus Read | Philip Yancey |

Made in the USA
Columbia, SC
30 August 2018